Technoism: At the Crossroads of Society and Technology

Beverly J. Davis

Acknowledgements

Thanks Val for the inspiration, the long hours of proof reading, for the hours of dialogue and most of all for the example you set for me every day.

I wish to thank my family and friends for their support through good times and bad times. I'll e-mail you ☺

In 1999, after many discussions with colleagues, I coined the term, "Technoism." I had noticed this unspoken phenomenon in my personal life and in my career. I wish to thank my colleagues for those long discussions over coffee, or other beverages, which inspired me to put all down on paper. I also thank all of my co-authors on various conference and journal papers, and the *Emerging Issues in Business and Technology* Conference/*Journal of Contemporary Business Issues* and Moira Gunn, host of NPR TechNation, for first allowing me to share my ideas.

Thanks to my students and the long class discussions on some of these topics.

Lastly, I wish to thank all those techno-illiterates for allowing me to offer a voice and the techno-savvy for paving the way for all of us to follow.

Forward

I am always amazed at the technological transformation we have experienced in the last ten years. This ongoing transformation has and will continue to change our lives. Some of us go willingly, others resist but follow hesitantly, others have not recognized the absolutism of our technological dependent society, and some are not educated or wealthy enough to entertain the thought. I, like so many, have a love-hate relationship with technology. E-mail is a gift and most of us could not imagine our lives without it. But we hate the SPAM and the time consumption associated with e-mail. The Internet is an unbelievable tool......literally the world at your fingertips. But the Internet is a threat to our personal privacy and can be used as a weapon as we discovered in our experiences with global terrorism. Technology has the power to accelerate us into the future but viruses, cyber-attacks and other techno-vulnerabilities gives technology the power to send us spinning backwards into the tunnel of the dark ages past. I only use my cell phone for quick calls yet I would be lost without its convenience. But I hate the lack of civility that cell phones have brought to our society. People lacking manners, carry cell phones allowing for phone ringing in movie theatres, restaurants, and other public spaces. And unbelievably, those same people inappropriately answer those phone calls speaking loudly for all to hear. And is there anyone living today who hasn't experienced "customer service" with automated telephone services? We dance with glee if selections offered by the robotic voice is a selection of choice and we do not have to wait on hold. Yet, we hate it because we can never seem to talk to "A REAL PERSON."

But with all of that said, Technoism is not really about the love-hate relationship we have with technology but about the freedom to voice dissent, the freedom to recognize the dark side of technology, and the freedom to express the parts we hate so we make it better for the future. Technoism is an unspoken and mostly unnoticed phenomenon, silencing the critics, suppressing the skepticism, and leading us to blind compliance. Technoism exists because we fear being ostracized or labeled old-fashioned or behind the times.

Recognition and rejection of Technoism is about feeling free to express the displeasure, refusing to accept poor quality, and objecting to the reliance of it in our lives. It is about slowing the pace of technology dependence in our society and evaluating, assessing, and analyzing the impacts. I have had many techno-savvy individuals object to my views and suggest that I am a Luddite or a Technophobe. Many perceptions are that I have waged a war on technological progression. I have been accused of fearing it because I don't understand it and I have been warned to get on board. This only reinforces my belief that it is not popular to express skepticism or criticize the technology revolution.

I had written and shared my views on Technoism at conferences and in journals for a few years and had received some resistance and some acknowledgement of the existence of this phenomenon. However, after my December, 2002 interview with Moira Gunn on the NPR talk show, TechNation, I started receiving e-mails and phone calls from all over the nation. I received requests for speaking engagements and many requests for the publication of this book. I found most individuals identified with the interview topic and recognized all or part of the interview discussion points as affecting their own lives. Many had observed the symptoms and recognized the phenomenon, so hearing my discussion on Technoism struck a chord because there had not been a word for it in the past. Many contacted me enthusiastically and many with thought-provoking ideas, sparked from some item during the interview. Technoism continues to stir the pot of controversy as this particular radio piece has apparently continually played over the nation on NPR stations.

I hope the reader will feel some reaction. This book will spark dissent, raise objection, and create laughter or concern. If it gets us to talk (hopefully in person), to question, and to celebrate, it has achieved the goal of slowing us down long enough to evaluate, assess, and analyze. ☺ reading!

TABLE OF CONTENTS

Technoism: At the Crossroads of Society and Technology

Introduction

Futurists predict quite an amazing digital world as we look ahead. Japan has been developing technology such as air conditioners that will kill the flu virus or refrigerators with cameras installed whereas one may check grocery supplies via a mobile phone while shopping at the market. Who could argue the benefits of Japan's new "automated closet" where a computer evaluates the weather conditions and picks your wardrobe for the day? However, the question one must ponder is, will these techno-wonders be functional next year? Next month? Next week? Consumers should feel betrayed, for the promises of improved customer service, time-savings, and ease of life have failed to surface, and in fact, the opposite seems to be true. Consumers have come to see the Old Economy products like automobiles, worked better at their very worst[58]. And people are stressed out more than ever before at a time when we counted on technology to make our lives easier. We are inundated with hundreds of e-mails, voice mail messages, and cell phone calls. Our lives are not necessarily easier with technology in our lives. We are on call 24/7 and always tethered to others. Although there are certainly customers who are indeed feeling betrayed, the reality is most consumers are still reluctant to admit technology isn't producing the customer service promised. There is stigma attached to those who dare question the benefits of technology in our lives. Who wishes to be labeled old-fashioned and behind the times? Who, but a few brazen journalists, would dare admit they are not getting the full use of their technology purchases? After all, if everyone else "is doing it" it must be 'me' with the problem, yes, the one with technological gadgets attached to my person, the one who has purchased every new technological toy and tool. Only with a red face do we sneak our technology purchases in our yard sale offerings, subjecting our technological purchases to the same fate as our unused exercise equipment.

Guilt, shame, and inexcusable are some of the words I think of when the desire moves me to speak of the short comings of this latest craze, called the Technology Revolution. How dare anyone challenge or refute the fact that technology is beneficial and we can improve anything by using the newest and most efficient technological tools. An employee, for example, could be ostracized for feeling that PDA's (Personal Data Assistants) are no more efficient than the old-fashioned hand written planner.

One may recognize a 1950's event, what we have come to know as McCarthyism, which produced the same level of shame and condemnation. We might compare this type of ostracization of innocent citizens to that felt by those accused of communism during the McCarthy era. Of course the madness that ensued during those days of finger pointing and name-calling was labeled McCarthyism. That same paranoia exists when anyone becomes a naysayer around the rapid conversion to technology gadgets. McCarthyism was an attitude that was based on fear and guilt. The intimidation that forced conformity averted any intellectual discussion on the rampant and unfounded accusations. The most neutral definition for McCarthyism is the force of conformity in order to avoid public condemnation. It can be applied in a broader sense as a tendency to suppress open communication. Today, individuals who have a valid realization of the overall and long-term effects of rapid and chaotic technological inundation are forced

into conformity as to avoid peer and public condemnation. At the 2001 *Emerging Issues*

in Business and Technology conference, the term Technoism was first introduced.

Technoism is the suppressed skepticism and blind compliance associated with the chaotic

and uncontrolled progression of technology in our lives. Therefore, the downside to

technological advancement is "not openly discussed" and freedom of speech is not

readily exercised. As someone once said: "We will never know how many books were

not written, movies were not made, songs were not sung, and paintings were not painted

as a result of McCarthyism." Will we someday look back at Technoism in the same way?

Does Technoism silence the critics? The critics that could help advance technology with

guidelines rather than uncontrolled and chaotic progression, the critics who challenge

technological advancement so that we can advance ethically and morally. Who will

challenge this fast-paced and uncontrolled phenomenon if Technoism is allowed to

flourish? Does anyone, as an unconvinced participant in the technology craze, dare admit

his or her true feelings about technology? Of course not, for few wish to be labeled

"fearful of change."

Any criticism of technological progression is immediately classified under

Luddite. Supposedly, in 1779, a man named Ned Ludd, an English laborer, destroyed

weaving machinery due to a belief that such machinery would diminish employment and

lower wages. An updated definition of Luddite according to current dictionaries is: "any

person opposed to technological advances, especially those designed to replace human

skill and experience with automated machinery." Let us not confuse Technoism with

Luddites or technophobia as Technoism is not a fear of technology but rather is a fear of condemnation for not conforming to the accepted ideology that technology is the be all and end all of American culture. Edward R. Murrow, on the television show, "See It Now," profiled Senator McCarthy and reminded viewers; "We must not confuse dissent with disloyalty." Similarly, Technoism (silenced dissent) is not to be confused with disloyalty (technophobia or Ludditism). Technoism silences dissent creating a dichotomy; get on board or be left behind. It is clear to see that most of these issues discussed are due to, not technology itself, but human exploitation through the use of technology. Experienced and knowledgeable marketing professionals constantly bombard us with advertisements attempting to convince the unsuspecting public that they can't survive without the latest technological tool. The media blitz is so convincing that we are "tricked" into buying every new electronic toy, persuaded it is a must for surviving in this fast paced life we lead.

In mythology, the Trickster represents anything that confuses fact with fiction. The Trickster views the world as opportunity for artifice and a land of opportunity for re-creation when it suits his purpose for manipulating others[84]. Trickster surely sees the inundation of technology in our lives as the ultimate opportunity: an opportunity for fooling an unsuspecting public. The absolutism of technology as a survival necessity is evident in marketing schemes. Marketing convinces us we must have the latest gadgets and "time-savers." Clever marketing convinces us we are losing out and falling behind if we do not invest in the latest technological wonders.

As stated previously, Technoism is the suppressed skepticism and blind compliance associated with the chaotic and uncontrolled progression of technology in our lives. The Trickster convinces the unsuspecting public that they will fall behind if they do not purchase the latest technological gadget. Technoism silences the critics of uncontrolled technological progression for fear of condemnation or being ostracized by the techno-savvy. Ahhh, yes, Technoism is the Trickster's friend. Trickster convinces human beings that technology can transform the chaotic into a normalizing and comforting illusion[90]. Technology marketing professionals have normalized an acceptance of poor product quality, expensive gadgets outdated at time of purchase, technology purchases needed to utilize previous technology purchases, and lacking customer service. Marketing campaigns offer comforting illusion by promising technology to save time, technology to help us gain power and control over our lives, and technologically enhanced customer service. The Trickster convinces us technology offers a normalizing of chaos when in actuality technology is the cause of the chaos in our lives.

The Trickster works his charm on individuals, workplaces, and society at large. Looking back on McCarthyism, one can see that no part of society was left untouched. Companies such as General Electric, General Motors, CBS, The New York Times, New York City of Education, and the United States Auto Workers followed Hollywood's example and fired employees for being "communists."[73] In fact, very few companies did *not* fire people during this era. Anyone who did not fit "standards" was fired. Today, workers are thrust into the technological world while silently accepting employers insistence they carry beepers, cell phones, carry laptops to check e-mail and regularly check voice mail. Refusal to do so would most certainly take someone off the fast track if not out the door. In its day, McCarthyism became the tool to punish people for things they had not done, punish people for things they might do, and ostracize anyone in society who dared state unpopular political opinion or take unpopular stances against such things, for example, as equal rights for black Americans[73]. An unpopular stance today may be the digital divide, which is a silent threat to many of our citizens. The tech-savvy or the "early adopters" in marketing lingo, are jumping ahead of society in largely proportional bounds, leaving the working class further and further behind. One attribute of the digital divide, technological language barriers, is threatening to dig the technologically challenged even deeper into a hole. The average person is unable to communicate in the technological jargon that is used by the upper echelon of technological circles. Many find it difficult to communicate even in the simplest of technological terms.

A study of Semiotics, or the study of hidden American cultural system signs and codes, shows us that Americans look to status symbols to mark off social success and identify the possessors' place in social hierarchy and for the purpose of our discussion, technological knowledge seems to be the great divide. Working class Americans are seemingly becoming less literate over time, however the bar has been raised on literacy standards we expect them to achieve and literacy definition now includes technological knowledge. The inflation on workplace literacy definition and the downward spiral of the poor and working class serves as a small-scale model of society and warns us of things to come. Technoism, as McCarthyism before it, silences the public debate on this facet of technological progress as the digital divide grows wider and wider.

Technology has and will continue to positively impact our lives; however, human exploitation found in marketing schemes shows us the dark side of the technological world. President Gerald Ford once said, "The American wage earner knows that a government big enough to give you everything you want is a government big enough to take from you everything you have." This can be applied to technological control of our lives as well. Technological advancements and progression gives us everything we wish for; convenience, for example. But the inundation of technology in our lives could also be viewed as big enough to negatively impact our valued time, relationships, health, and careers. Technoism silences those who observe this facet of society for fear of being ostracized. The Trickster's usage of Technoism gives the public or users of technology a false sense of power and control over their lives when in fact they are losing more and more control. Ever hear of a CEO, due to massive e-mail barrage, creating a position and hiring a person just to control and maintain the e-mail management and correspondence?

As previously stated, social issues must be considered, as well. Technoism silences those who question the growing digital divide while more and more working class Americans struggle to survive in their increasingly digital world. Children living in households without computers, enter K-12 classrooms poorly equipped and immediately behind. In the race for lifetime skill development, these children are placed at the same starting line as those technologically-gifted children and expected to equally contend. By the time they graduate, they can only watch the winners cross the line of success as they lag behind. And senior citizens struggle to understand the simplest of technology tools; tools that at times are needed to function as more and more services migrate to the Internet.

One must not view this discussion as putting technology in a negative light, for it is my belief that most of the issues discussed in this book are due to "unintended consequences." Adam Smith, an early economist, introduced this concept that most actions and decisions will result in unintended consequences. Although he mostly applied this to government actions, it most certainly fits our discussion here on technology. Technology is a gift, but Trickster and his friend Technoism hide in the void between intended consequences and unintended consequences. This is where they are most effective.

This book will look to expose the Trickster so to eliminate the power of Technoism in our lives. It will offer some suggestions on positive technological progression, best coupled with open assessment. We will look at communication, ethics, trust, and privacy issues. We will explore Technoism at work, at home, in the workplace, at school, and in society as a whole.

Part 1: Trickster and his friend, Technoism

- ➢ **Consumer Conformity and Business not as Usual**

- ➢ **Technology on Technology: T-on-T**

- ➢ **Normalizing and Comforting Illusions**

- ➢ **Snapshots in Time: Technological Imagery**
  - o **Trusting Digital Historical Information**
  - o **A Loss of Culture**

- ➢ **Business Sense or Technoism?**
  - o **Leadership and Technology**
  - o **Stress in the Workplace**
  - o **Ethics and Technology**

Consumer Conformity and Business that is not as Usual

In American society, competition and climbing the ladder of success is the sign you have arrived. In the business world, the ladder of success is full of climbers who conform and assimilate. The Trickster exposes this facet of life in the United States and depends on Technoism to guilt ladder-climbers into the acceptance of the chaos associated with technological invasion in our lives. The media blitz convinces the public they need every technological tool to stay in the loop. Technological tools are always touted as newer and faster and better. However, Walter Kirn, Time Magazine compared Old Economy Products with New Economy Products when he said, "One-inch-thick steel would only be one-inch thick on weekend nights and holidays. During weekday business hours, it would only be one-third of an inch; and if one carried the steel outside one's own area, it would cost six times as much. Refrigerators would chill eggs and butter for only three or four hours before they crashed entailing a call to an 800 number."[58]
In the past, quality and durability was an expectation and the idea that a product would come with restrictions would be laughable.

Marketing experts are familiar with marketing cycles. The marketing cycle typically means the newest products in the market are quickly snatched up by the "early adopters" or the innovators. Later adopters, or the majority, wait until products have become mainstream and proven before purchase. Of course by that time products are less expensive and the kinks have been ironed out. Late adopters typically force the prices down and force improvement of quality just by waiting. This market pattern is expected in the study of product acquisition. But with technology, the cycle never completes. Late adopters are waiting side-by-side with the early adopters so as to stay in the technological loop. Quality product improvement is not part of this new shortened acquisition cycle. Rather than improving the quality and lowering the costs to meet the majority's needs, customer satisfaction is sacrificed for a continuous flow of "gotta have" technological gadgets. The mystery lies with the late adopters. In the past, these consumers have proven to consistently wait until the product is proven, less expensive, and more convenient. But these concerns are abandoned when the spell of Trickster and Technoism causes these usually cautious consumers to buy poor quality, products out-of-date at time of purchase, and products with no promise of customer service. The gleeful Trickster is joyful as these late adopters buy more and more technology to "upgrade" attributing poor product quality and functioning to their own technological ignorance. Many of these late adopters are working persons struggling to stay in the workplace loop.

Unfortunately, Technoism silences the ambitious in business that is wired to the office 24/7, creates an acceptance of technologically driven invasion of personal time, and leads to blind compliance fueled by the idealism that it is a new economy business necessity to be connected to work through technology. Here the Trickster tricks us twice. Employees, who are convinced to be available through technology at all hours, do so when business informs them it is to serve the customer so the business can survive. Yet, customer service is at an all-time low. Technology has actually moved customer service a step backwards[34]. Although companies continue to boast the customer is king, the American Consumer Service Index is down to 72.9% and customer service has become a tangle of telephones, e-mail, and websites; Technology has removed the need for qualified customer service representatives to discuss customer concerns.[34] The computer can now literally guide a non-qualified representative through a set of pre-designed questions ultimately answering the customer complaint. The fallacy is that one of the pre-designed computer responses will answer the customer's questions. Technology has also allowed companies to outsource work or consolidate their operations in several different geographical locations. PC World recently surveyed readers about PC support[35]. The 27,000 respondents showed satisfaction at an all-time low. The complaints centered on longer waits on hold and less knowledgeable technicians. Technoism flourishes; however, as the public has become so dependent on technology advancements, acceptance of poor service has become a fact of life. Ellen Goodman, a national syndicated columnist, complained recently that it has come to the point where average Americans of average age need tech support just to run their daily lives. She noted that every "upgrade" now downgrades the quality of life. She complained the more functional, the more dysfunctional[43]. Companies are selling complex products to low-end consumers (late adopters).[35] Ellen Goodman recently admitted to being one of the "low-end" consumers. She hoped to buy a new television but the new televisions come fully equipped with the "options from hell." Goodman sarcastically remarked that watching television now requires the training and skill of a pilot at the controls of an Airbus 300. A Dell Computer representative reported they were seeing a lot more novice users becoming part of their customer base (again, late adopters)[51]. He commented that it sets an even higher need for assistance because computers are becoming more complex. Yet, as aforementioned, customer service at many companies may be deteriorating. In fact, at the Austin, Texas Better Business Bureau where Dell computer is based, it was reported

that the BBB received 1,195 complaints on Dell Tech support for the period of October-

March, 2001 up from 616 in the six months before[57]. Could it be the service departments

of these technology centers are designed for the early adopters, the consumers with little

need for assistance?

Ellen Goodman suggested, instead of forcing consumers to fit the equipment,

technology makers need to make the equipment fit the consumer. But what motivation

would marketers have to do this? If the low-end consumers are upgrading to "keep up"

and new technology is purchased to manage old technology, "creeping complication," as

Goodman labels it, will continue to benefit technology producers and marketers.

Remember, the newest and greatest technological innovations have always been designed

specifically for the early adopter, the technological savvy. But with the late adopters

lining up to purchase the newest technological innovations, the complications will

continue to frustrate consumers. Consumers, in the eagerness to tame the technological

frontier, continue to purchase technological upgrades and in some cases, newer

technologies are purchased for the sole purpose of managing already existing technology

purchases.

Technology-on-Technology

The "buying up" idealism can be observed when looking at "Technology-on-Technology" (T-on-T) purchases. The Trickster uses the myth of progress when marketers convince one needs T-on-T to make lives even faster and more efficient by managing existing technologies. There isn't a better example of this than the e-mail system. A recent study by Pitney Bowes found the average worker, from receptionist to CEO, handles an average of 204 messages a day in the form of e-mail, answering machine messages and voice-mail messages[53]. In a recent *USA Today* Report entitled, "E-mail avalanche even buries CEOs," it was found most CEO's praise the efficiency of e-mail but curse its inefficiency. One CEO complained that he spends three to four hours a day sorting through e-mail. Another CEO interviewed admitted he deletes 80% of his e-mails without reading them. But many CEO's and managers today are hiring administrative assistants just to sort through e-mails. New wireless technology (T-on-T) now ties these CEOs and others to the office after hours. With the use of wireless technology, many CEO's confessed to handling business e-mails at home on their own time. The USA Today article warned the exploding use of wireless e-mail devices is behind the coming swell of more e-mail. This, of course, creates a need for T-on-T-on-T to manage the explosion of the additional e-mail created through T-on-T. According to BWCS Consulting, 75% of corporate e-mail subscribers will be transmitted via wireless devices by 2006. Even Congress is feeling overwhelmed. In the year 2000, The House was hit with more than 50 million e-mails up from two million in 1998 and the Senate received nearly 27 million messages in 2000, fifteen times as many as in 1996[72]. Again, many lawmakers admit to deleting at least half of those e-mails without reading them. Senator Hillary Rodham Clinton alone gets 8000 e-mails a day (may be higher now with her new book and potential presidential candidate rumors). And the inundation of SPAM, or unwanted advertising, on our computer systems has increasingly busied the daily E-mailer. A recent report by Forrester Research warned that unwanted messages or SPAM is expected to triple this year[96].

In Europe, a law protects e-mailers from unsolicited junk E-mail. Japan, too, has laws prohibiting SPAM junk mail. The United States, unfortunately, does not have such laws. There have been bills pending and increasing concern but nothing has materialized. Some states have laws but mostly, SPAMMERS are free to inundate our E-mail addresses with junk mail. On a typical day, Hotmail subscribers collectively receive more than one billion pieces of junk E-mail[55]. Such SPAM accounts for 80% of messages received-not including mail blocked by Hotmail's first line of filters[55]. A recent news article reported that at AT&T WorldNet a year ago about a dozen out of every 100 messages were SPAM. Today its closer to 20-25 – on top of another 200 or 300 E-mails sent to invalid accounts by SPAMMERS trying to guess addresses. Why is SPAM expected to increase? SPAMMERS are sending out higher volumes because filters are better at blocking messages and the SPAMMERS send out more and cleverly find ways to evade filters[55]. And SPAMMING is fairly cheap, SPAMMERS paying less than a penny per pitch.

Massive E-Mails, SPAMMERS, Wireless Technology.....the Trickster mixes things up again as marketers claim technology will save time and help us to gain power and control over our increasingly technologically-controlled lives.

Normalizing and Comforting Illusions

The feeling of having no control or power over circumstances can be frightening to most of us. The influx of technology in our lives promised to make our lives easier and more manageable. In other words, technology was implemented in our lives to give us more power over and more control over our time. Technological communication devices such as e-mail and voice mail were embraced and touted as mainstreaming of our communications. Personal Data Assistants (PDAs) and other electronic planning devices were promoted by marketers as the efficient method of organization. Automated operator systems were designed to improve customer service so we could spend less time "on hold." Laptop computers promised us 24/7 "take home work" capabilities so we could gain control of our work projects. Technology has transitioned us into a "knowledge" era where information is at the fingertips of anyone, anywhere, anytime. Somewhere during this massive transformation, technology managed to gain the control over our lives. The very tools we embraced to help us maintain power and control in our lives has turned on us and it now has the control and power over us. The Trickster, found in marketing ploys, turned the table on us when we were busy answering e-mails. Where e-mail has increasingly complicated our lives, new technology purchases are touted as the next best thing to time management. Many of the aforementioned CEOs, who felt the massive e-mail deluge out of control, predicted that instant messaging and virtual private networks (VPSs) could slow the growth of e-mail. Again, the Trickster offers hope to today's management by giving them the illusion of control through faster and more efficient time management. And Technoism puts fear in the hearts of those who question whether faster technology is the answer to the stress in their lives. Technoism is the Trickster's friend, silencing the critics and allowing technology producers and marketers to trick the public into faster and faster lifestyles. Marketers are now offering the illusion of more control over our lives as technological communications are now found in our vehicles with dashboard PCs. We can now take work home and work on our way home. Problem with too many e-mails? Switch to instant messaging and make communications even faster. Too many voice mails? Then purchase the Voice Mail Notification System.

The Trickster, through cleverly and exploitive marketing schemes, convinces us that one must have the newest and best technological gadget. The Trickster uses Technoism to silence the critics when digital purchases offer less than quality and customer service satisfaction. The Trickster goes one step further and convinces the unsuspecting public they must have the newest technological gadget to supplement the previous technological gadget to stay in the loop. The Trickster is evident in the workplace, invading our personal lives, while Technoism silences under the pretense of career progression. Ever see the person at the airport, taking cell phone call after another? These people are overheard to brag about how "busy" they are as if it is a badge of honor. Watch the career climber in action at the airport. Once, as I awaited a delayed flight, I, and everyone in the same section of the airport, listened to a woman on her cell phone talk to person after person, lamenting about her busy schedule and resulting lack of sleep. Of course, she talked loudly so as to be heard over the noise of the airport. It was painful to hear this story told over and over again in such detail. If my flight had been delayed a minute longer, I may have asked her why she didn't turn her cell phone off and utilize her downtime for sleep. Another time and airport, I listened to a man discuss business in such

detail, I think I could have managed his business in his absence. Another time I watched a

fast-track man flying with his family, apparently on vacation. He sat next to me with his

young daughter and his wife sat a few rows back with their young son. The little girl

fidgeted and demanded attention while her father handled business with one phone call

after another. He, as so many other "trendsetters," turned on his PDA immediately when

he was told to turn off his cell phone for take-off. He plugged away until we reached

cruising altitude at which time he pulled out his laptop and worked with it the remainder

of the flight. Meanwhile, the little girl finally fidgeted herself to sleep. As soon as the

plane landed, he had his cell phone on again, checking the newest and most current news

at the office. The image is of a technologically-savvy person, in-the-loop, and on the fast

track in life. But sometimes images can be deceiving as we find when we conduct an

authenticity test on Internet images.

Snapshots in time or Technological Imagery

Research suggests one in ten college students have turned in a research or term paper downloaded in its entirety from the Internet. This is a booming business on the Web as can be seen when researching this topic. In 1989, California, one of the seventeen states prohibiting the sale of term papers, sued the owners of Research Assistance, a California-based term paper vendor[70]. The result was a $50,000 fine but this only caused this company to relocate. The company's co-founder sold it two years ago for fewer than one million dollars and the new owner advertises in Rolling Stone Magazine and calls its term papers, "unpublished research papers." With technological progression come questionable ventures. Wendy Conklin, Editor of the *Diversity Factor*, noted recently that ethics is having a difficult time keeping up with fast-paced technological advancements. Ms. Conklin, in the Winter 2001, *Diversity Factor*, offered some examples of technological illusion:

> ➤ In October 2000, the University of Wisconsin altered a photo for its undergraduate admissions booklet in an effort to appear more diverse to prospective students. The head of an African-American student was superimposed among an all-white crowd, but the sun shone only on his face and not on the others in the crowd, highlighting the deception.

> ➤ Also that October, a computer technician at the University of Idaho replaced the heads of two white students in a photo on its web site, to

create the appearance of a more diverse student body. The staff caught the change and removed the photo.

- ➤ In 1996, the British unit of Ford Motor Company apologized for replacing the faces and hands of minority employees with white faces and hands in a photo.

- ➤ In June of 2001, the Screen Actors Guild mounted a protest against Ford Motor Company alleging that a white stunt double in a Lincoln Mercury commercial was given a "paint down" in the absence of an African American suitable for the part. Both Lincoln Mercury and its advertising agency, Young & Rubicam, denied the accusation, but agreed to suspend production until the actor's strike was settled.

Conklin reminded us of recent news media blunders as well:

- ➤ The August 26-September 1, 1989 issue of *TV Guide* featuring Oprah Winfrey on its cover next to a pot of gold. Winfrey's face had been superimposed on actress Ann-Margaret's body.

- ➤ The 1994 photo of O.J. Simpson appearing on the cover of *Time* magazine. At the time, Simpson was the lead suspect in his wife's murder case. *Time* magazine was criticized for going too far when it darkened his face.

➢ The January 16, 1989 *Newsweek* photo of Tom Cruise and Dustin Hoffman promoting their movie *Rain Man*. The actors were photographed separately in New York and Hawaii, and the two photographs were composited together. Neither the caption nor photo credit indicated this was anything but a conventional portrait.

➢ The cover of the February 16, 1994 issue of *New York Newsday*, on which rival skaters Tonya Harding and Nancy Kerrigan appeared in an image combining two existing photos to create a fictional moment in the future. The manipulation was acknowledged as a "composite illustration."

Whether you are a teacher concerned about student deceit in research activities or a participant in popular culture, technology is the great imposter substituting technological imagery for reality. This fact became glaringly real when individuals attempted to digitally alter the famous September 11, 2001 photograph showing three firefighters raising the American flag over the rubble of destruction. This photograph was symbolic of American resolve at that point in time and it was shared worldwide as a symbol of America's strength and fortitude. When it was suggested the photograph serve as a possible model for a memorial at Ground Zero, someone changed the images of three white firefighters to include a diverse grouping of firefighters. Anything involving

September 11, 2001 and Ground Zero aroused great emotion during those times and many Americans emotionally reacted to this alteration suggestion as disrespectful and unrealistic.

We rely on photographs and written accounts to preserve our memories of past time. Columnist Ellen Goodman, in her editorial, *Lack of Trust can be by-product of new technology*, offered the following question for thought: "If we can't believe what we see, will we see only what we already believe?"[43] Goodman warned the same technology which informs us can also misinform us and disinform us. She asked, "who will draw the line between truth and propaganda?" Goodman offered more examples sharing a recent example of technological wizardry. When producers of the movies, *Serendipity* and *Zoolander* wanted to get rid of the Twin Towers backdrop, they simply deleted the image. On sitcoms and in movies, the advertisers who pay the most for product placement will see their product magically appear in an already pre-taped episode. And, scientists at MIT have created the first realistic videos that can show people saying things they never actually said. The most recent revelation involved the front cover of a national magazine. It was admitted that the magazine took the head of actress Julia Roberts and superimposed another body. Why would one need to change Julia Robert's body? I suppose, because they can.

Other than the brave journalists with job descriptions requiring critical analysis, Technoism silences those of us who question the lack of ethical assessment of technological advancement. When one looks back on time at his or her ancestors through black and white photographs, it is assumed that what one sees is the real image. We study those old photographs, nostalgic and reflective of our ancestors, to identify with our history. Many of us have had our portraits taken at a photography studio and appreciate the "touch-ups" we see on the computer allowing us to take home a false image of ourselves to display proudly on our walls. But when technology tricks our reality and makes it difficult to separate fact and fiction, a lack of trust permeates our society. Not only must we question incoming information and image, we must question the reliability of technology to store our historical information and the documentation of original historical news through databases.

Trusting Digital Historical Information

Technoism suppresses skepticism and allows the technological explosion to progress without contemplative analysis and assessment. Locally, I have witnessed a debate through the media that most likely is found in small communities nationwide. In South Bend, IN recently, local history buffs voiced concerns over the library's plans to computerize historical documents. The plan was to digitalize all the information in the Local History Room in the main library. The library director said the library plans to scan in all existing newspaper clippings, books, and other fragile historic documents and make the material available via a computerized database at the library[37]. Some of the concerns expressed: would the computer illiterate be able to access information? In other words, would the public information offered at the library be available to a diverse population (Classes of technological literacy)? What will happen to the files in the future? Will digital records be considered valid by organizations requiring written documentation of ancestry? Although the library insists they will keep originals in locked storage in the basement, historically, libraries have been known to discard this storage after several years. In a recent book, *Double Fold: Libraries and the Assault on Paper,* author Nicholson Baker wrote that some of the world's greatest libraries-including the Library of Congress-have betrayed a public trust by selling off or discarding irreplaceable collections of original books and newspapers after they were microfilmed or digitally scanned[37].

One concern about storing all historical, personal, and business information on database is the fear of technology failure. Although computers and databases are used for our daily lives, when it comes to trusting them to store our information reliably there is doubt. Computers are at the heart of every aspect of our lives today. Dependence upon information created by computers and networks is like dependence on foreign oil: What happens when access is cut off?[25] Charles K. Davis in a 2001 article, *Planning for the Unthinkable: IT Contingencies,* warned that modern business can no longer function without its information technology (IT) infrastructure. Davis cautioned technological dependence is serious business. "One only needs to reflect back to the eruption of Mt. St. Helens, or the bombings of the World Trade Center in New York and the Federal Building in Oklahoma City, or the earthquakes in San Francisco, hurricanes on the Gulf Coast (not to mention tornadoes, floods, fires, computer viruses, and disgruntled employees) to appreciate the risk involved."[25] This article was written before the tragic September 11, 2001 World Trade Center and Pentagon catastrophes. In our grief, it didn't

seem appropriate to consider business losses. But the fact remains, on September 11,
2001, hundreds of businesses lost resources stored in databases and lost intellectual
capital creating huge vacuums in business record-keepings and business operations.
Davis said that if a firm's data center is destroyed, insurance will pay for the facilities lost
and maybe some business interruption losses, but without network systems and
databases, the firm will not be able to conduct its business. Recently, a hacker created a
fast-moving worm that disrupted computers worldwide. This worm, "LovSan," exploited
a security hole in Microsoft systems. The hacker included a hidden message: "billy gates
why do you make this possible? Stop making money and fix your software." This glitch
caused embarrassment at Microsoft as they frantically issued "patches" for the security
hole. This invasion gives us pause as we evaluate the fallibility of our data systems. In
addition, the recent "Northeast Blackout of 2003" should raise red flags. When a major
power grid malfunctioned, electricity went out from Detroit to Clevelend and into
Canada. New York City was included in this power outage which lasted two days in
some areas. There was enough blame to go around, but most finger-pointing has been
directed at the malfunctioning computerized systems. During the recent Iraq war,
technology was used on the battlefield. Upon his return home, one soldier stated that he
documented on paper as well. He made a telling statement when he said, " ….a bullet in a
notebook is a hole, a bullet in a computer is destruction of all documentation."
Contingency Plans are suggested by Davis, but he also shared that most businesses
hesitate to invest major dollars for something that may never happen. He offered Y2K as
an example of companies that spent money on contingency plans only to have Y2K
sound a false alarm.

Y2K could be considered a warning for all of us, however. The fallibility of our digitalized documentation was evident when the public was warned of this potential catastrophe. Of course the Trickster used this opportunity to terrify the public into purchasing Y2K protection software. Warnings of entire government systems failing and technological networks shutting down penetrated our news. On New Years Eve, 1999, televisions broadcast across the world as we watched each time zone enter the new millennium without a glitch. The world was frozen for several hours and when it was found the emergency had passed, life went on. Trickster, with the Y2K promotion past, quickly diverted attention to the urgency of the new millennium. Technoism continued to silence the critics as marketers began touting new and improved technological gadgetry for the new millennium. The Trickster and his friend Technoism found a new platform once the potential Y2K threat passed. Trickster began a campaign of new century thinking to get the general public back to the marketplace. Trickster used his friend Technoism to increase the pressure for skeptics to silence their cries as new and improved technology was introduced and promoted. After all, who wants to be accused of not keeping up with the new millennium? Who wants to be labeled old-fashioned in the year 2000?

A Loss of Culture

In his book, *Cultural Amnesia*, Stephen Bertman warned of a loss of culture in America. One topic of concern is the computerization of historical books and records. His major concern is the fact there are fewer and fewer traces of our past and therefore less incentive to remember or value what once was. Mr. Bertman noted although this is the "information age" we are actually losing history because of either decay of the fragile materials on which it is inscribed or the rapid obsolescence of technology needed to understand it. He cited UNESCO research: "three-quarters of the films made worldwide before the 1950's have already disappeared."[4] And magnetic tapes have an average life span of ten years, microfilm has an average life span of 100 years, and after five years, CD-ROMS are either unreadable or unreliable. Another issue brought forth in this book is the short life-span of computers hardware and software. Computers store masses of information but without equipment to encode it, the digital information is useless. Compatibility between computer systems has always been a concern in the electronic age, but what happens when valuable information is lost when information stored on old equipment is not compatible with a new system?

Recently there was an editorial discussing a discovery by a British gentleman. He discovered a letter hand-written by Captain James Cook written approximately 231 years ago and addressed to the British Admiralty with the first news of his safe return from a three year explorational trip. The editorial, originally printed in the *Los Angeles Times*, criticized our electronic world today by comparing such a find to today's digital record-keeping. The author sarcastically suggested Captain Cook would have sent an e-mail or inserted his memoirs on a web page. And most likely, the e-mails would be deleted, the web page updated and those old historical letters would be permanently destroyed as we do so "routinely and ruthlessly" in our society today. Technological advancements have allowed us to live in the moment, communicating quickly and electronically. Will future generations have a history on which to reflect?

Some futurists go so far as to predict the demise of writing. Geoffrey Meredith believes text will all but disappear as electronic books, graphic novels, and voice-recognition software edge out written language. He predicts by the year 2070, "the only people using text as literature (as opposed to information transmission) will be an elite and mostly very elderly priesthood, for whom it will be an arcane art form-sort of like the sonnet or haiku today."[67] He predicts that fifty years from now, books, newspapers, and magazines will be relics of the past. The Trickster has convinced many to document all records and historical documents with technology while Technoism silences but a few who are viewed as alarmists. The Trickster offers a new and bright world in technology where one must jump on board or be left behind while his friend Technoism guilts those who relish historical books and text into silent acceptance of "change." The Trickster is really tricking upcoming generations as the future may hold no historical data for them and the information that does filter through may be altered and unreliable.

Business Sense or Technoism:

Leadership

The discipline of leadership has been studied for ages. Year after year, books are

written offering suggestions on how to manage in a fast-paced, chaotic world of work.

Technology has indeed made the manager's job more adaptable and flexible. However,

today leaders either substitute technology for interpersonal communication with

employees or they seek quick and easy solutions for communicating with employees in

person. Many businesspersons remember "The One-Minute Manager," a book written in

the 1980's that encouraged techniques for properly treating people. The message of the

book to managers was to take one minute to praise a person, one minute to set goals with

that person, and one minute to reprimand your employees when necessary. I always felt

the premise of the book was on target, however, I always questioned the suggestion that a

manager spend one minute on these very important tasks involving employees. It takes

much longer, I argued. But technology has once again taken us to new levels. Mark

Breier, CEO and president at software seller Beyond.com, has published the book,

"The10-second Internet Manager: Survive, Thrive & Drive your Company in the

Information Age." Mr. Breier suggests that one-minute is too long and offers tips in his

book about moving fast, using e-mail, and building a culture to speed up your company[48].

It is a nightmare to think of how many companies are now hiring, firing, and even

conducting performance appraisals via technology thus avoiding personal

communication. A subscription website, PerformanceReview.com, now exists so that

companies who belong can go to the service's special template and fill in the information on employees[20]. The service's mainframe generates a concise evaluation that incorporates the reviewer's comments. One company mentioned in the article remarked that since every review is this same short format, each takes about three minutes to cover and the company has reduced the time spent on the process by 60-70%. Of course they have most likely cut the communication and interpersonal interaction with employees by 60-70% as well.

Stress in the Workplace

"We're on the verge of a technological backlash. The irony of wireless technologies, designed to untether business professionals and executives from their desks, is that they increasingly tether these increasingly tense individuals to technology" (Hymowitz & Silverman, *Wall Street Journal*)

Today's stress is, in many ways, about too much information coming from too many sources and the loss of control that instills[53]. Hymowitz and Silverman shared a survey by Pitney Bowes of some 1200 workers from receptionists to chief executives at top companies and found that employees handle an average of 204 messages a day, counting e-mail, voice mail, snail mail and memos. A recent insertion in *Fast Company* shared the following statistics:

The typical U.S. office worker:

- ➢ Has six interruptions every hour

- ➢ Receives an average of 52 phone calls a day

- ➢ Receives an average of 36 e-mails a day

- ➢ Receives an average of 23 voice mails a day

- ➢ Receives an average of 18 pieces of postal mail a day

- ➢ Receives an average of 18 interoffice memos a day

- ➢ Receives an average of 14 faxes a day

- ➢ Is paged an average of 8 times a day

- ➢ Receives an average of 4 cell phone calls a day

Is it any wonder that reports of stress are at an all time high? Today's stress is, in many ways, about too much information coming from too many sources-and the loss of control that instills[53]. The aforementioned *Wall Street Journal* article, "Can Workplace Stress Get Worse?" discussed overworked and stress-filled workers. One person remarked that you never feel done and technological tools like e-mail and cell-phones, tools designed to make life easier, has tethered him to work and usurped his private life. Another astonishing fact, found in a recent 2002 survey conducted by *American Demographics,* tells us 69% of 1300 full-time working adults admit to staying in contact with the office while on vacation (see previous airport story).

The tech tools available-from credit card size cell phones to wireless PDA organizers, has in turn made us reachable anytime, anywhere. The *Wall Street Journal* article discussed the changed life of a young executive, a chief operating officer of an online human-resource company. He told them that he used to listen to music in his car driving to and from work but now he talks on his cell phone with clients while he drives and although e-mail enables him to communicate more quickly than he once did with faxes and letters, the volume of messages he sends and receives has increased his workload by 30% in the last three years, he estimated. These authors concluded that there is an extreme amount of stimulation at work that can leave one feeling exhausted. Others interviewed in the article complained that the constant communication affects personal privacy.

Information overload has replaced information scarcity as an important new emotional, social, and political problem[32]. And stress is a common phenomenon in the Information Age. It contributes to cardiovascular disease, depression, and gastro-intestinal disorders. The National Mental Health Association reposts that 75% to 90% of all visits to physicians are stress-related. A study conducted by the National Sleep Foundation found that in the last five years, Americans have tended to work more and sleep less. While the amount of sleep Americans get has gone down in these last five years, the number of hours worked has gone up[77]. Let us not blame this new fast-paced life entirely on technology, although it is technology that has made our lives faster. It is a people-problem when instant gratification becomes an expectation. Have you ever been frustrated when your computer wasn't fast enough? Have you cursed and tapped your fingers on the table in disgust when the fax did not arrive soon enough? We have grown accustomed to fast, speedy, overnight, and instant satisfaction. We not only have grown accustomed to it, we demand it and become frustrated when we are not instantly gratified.

But put in perspective, continuous communication with work and the office is an invasion of privacy that is tolerated under the guise of technological advancement. Technoism has allowed stressed employees to accept and tolerate employer abuse that has taken years of legislation to prevent. Employees are "on duty" 24 hours a day because of technological advances. The general public, due to the fear of Technoism, accepts this information overload. Why else would people put up with being paid for a 40 hour week yet be on duty for 24 hours a day? Out-Look programs even tell companies where we are and when we can be scheduled for a meeting. Employees blindly comply because of Technoism. In 1938, the Fair Labor Standards Act was passed establishing laws outlining minimum wage, overtime pay, and maximum hour requirements for most U.S. workers. With the technologically controlled workplace today, it seems as though this law is being considerably violated and should be reconsidered and updated to protect today's workforce. As it is, Trickster and his friend Technoism has silenced and fooled some workers into feeling a false sense of importance as they add clips to their belt loops allowing availability to the workplace during personal time.

A good example of this can be found in Silicon Valley where status is directly proportional to the number of gadgets secreted about your person[62]. A recent news article described "today's fully accessorized geek" as wearing a belt so loaded down with stuff he looks like a handyman. On this utility belt is the digital trendsetter's cell phone, two-way pager, and of course the personal digital assistant (PDA). All of these "tools" keep the person on-line, on call, and in motion. In the world of Silicon Valley, this constant communication flow is disguised as technological savvy and a digital trendsetter wouldn't dare utter disparaging remarks. The role of leader in any organization today means to accept this invasion of privacy as part of the job description. If you are salaried, there is no limit to the invasion of privacy. I have a friend who started a new job and jokingly bragged about her new importance as she showed her two-way pager and beeper, cell-phone, her PDA planner, and her Blackberry. I would guess that by now the joke is on her.

There has been an epidemic of burnt out employees and employees seeking trimmed down hours at work. Many executives, who have "cut back" to 55 hours a week, find they may be cutting themselves out of the running for future promotions or career opportunities[29]. And, according to a study last year by the Women's Bar Association of Massachusetts, women attorneys who worked at private firms in the state said that reducing their hours hurt their relationships with colleagues, decreased their chances of getting satisfying assignments and ultimately derailed their goals of becoming a partner. Nearly 40% of respondents in that study who ultimately left their firms said that those sorts of negative implications about cutting back hours affected their decision to leave the firm[29].

Whether at work, at home, or on vacation, the corporate climber, even while complaining about the stress and increased workloads attributed to technological advancement, accepts each new and improved technological intrusion into their personal lives. The silence of Technoism is deafening allowing Trickster to exploit them as consumers one more time.

Ethics, Technology and the Workplace

New genetic research may make it possible to identify an individual's lifetime risk of cancer, heart attack, and other diseases and experts worry that this information could be used to discriminate in hiring, promotions, or insurance[88]. A recent news article acknowledged employers and insurers could save millions of dollars if they could use predictive genetics to identify in advance, and then reject, workers, or policy applicants who are predisposed to chronic disease. Thus, continues the article, genetic discrimination could join the list of other forms of discrimination: racial, ethnic, age, and sexual. The Medical Science field has recently published the human genome map and sequence that has enormous implications for improving the health and lives of many patients. However, there is widespread fear that an individual's genetic information will be used against them and this fear is affecting how people view the medical revolution promised by mapping the human genome. The Equal Employment Opportunity Commission (EEOC) filed its first lawsuit in February 2001, when a company was charged with conducting genetic testing on its employees without their permission. At least one worker was threatened with dismissal unless he agreed to the test[88]. A Time/CNN poll that found 75% of Americans surveyed did not want insurance

companies to know their genetic code and 84% wanted that information withheld from
the government[88]. Although no one has taken an employer or insurer to court for
discrimination on the basis of genetic bias, lawsuits are likely to surface soon[47]. In 1995,
the federal Equal Employment Opportunity Commission issued an interpretation of the
1990 Americans with Disabilities Act stating that workers should be protected from
genetic bias, but the issue hasn't been tested in courts[47]. There is a widespread fear that
genetic information will be used against individuals as most individuals fear losing their
privacy. This leads us into another technological dilemma: Technological snooping and
individual privacy.

Wouldn't it be wonderful to have an assistant who helped guide you through your
workday by making sure you didn't make too many typographical errors? What if that
same friend told your boss that you made personal phone calls or worse yet, told your
boss exactly what you said during the conversations? With friends like that, who needs
enemies, right? This "friend" is the technological devices that are used today to monitor
employees in the workplace. Currently, as many as 26 million workers in the United
States are monitored in their jobs, and this number will increase as computers are used
more and more within companies and the cost of these monitoring systems goes down[27].
Time and time again, the news is full of cases where employers were sued because they
had been eavesdropping or monitoring employee behavior. A 1993 study conducted by
"MacWorld" Magazine found that at companies with 1000 or more employees, 30% of
the firms had searched employee's computer files, electronic mail, and voicemail[46]. This
article claimed that an estimated 20 million Americans may be subject to electronic

monitoring through their computers and that doesn't include the use of telephones and video cameras that could boost the number to 50 million or more. In a 1999 survey by the American Management Association, 67% of 1054 companies reported that they use electronic monitoring and surveillance[9]. In six years the percentage increased 37%! Of those polled, 84% say they informed employees of surveillance policies. Up to now, there is no legislation that clearly defines this invasion and most court cases come down in favor of the employer. But the fact that employee monitoring is legal doesn't automatically make it right. *Business Ethics*, in 1999, described human beings in the workplace as more than cogs in a machine noting that human beings are entitled to respect requiring some attention to privacy. As long as companies use technology to monitor human work, some humans will react negatively to the procedure and demand protection through legislation and the issues will focus on management's desire to know "who is doing what" in the office and an employee's right to privacy and human dignity[27].

Technological advancements coupled with our society's litigious tendencies, has made the issue of privacy a focus of employers for several years. Employers are concerned about the content of e-mail messages sent from corporate computers and employees are concerned about their privacy to do so. Employers have been prying into their employees' e-mail messaging and Internet use now that there is software available to do so. Employers insist the need to monitor stems from the technological and legal realities of the newly wired workplace[96]. Recently, The New York Times fired 23 employees for e-mailing distasteful jokes[96]. And a survey conducted by the American Management Association found the following activities companies monitored:

- Internet Connections: 54%

- E-mail Messages: 38%

- Computer Files: 31%

- Job Performance via Video: 15%

- Phone Conversations: 12%

- Voice-mail Messages: 7%

With technology permeating our work lives, legal questions remain unaddressed. With the changing and more flexible workplace, we sometimes find telecommuters working at home but using company equipment. Courts will be asked to draw boundaries over the next year or two as these issues grow[55]. Those telecommuters equal approximately 28 million Americans or one in five employees. Legal experts warn as long as you are interfacing with office or office equipment, there should be the assumption there are no privacy rights[55]. But, the National Labor Relations Board would tend to disagree. The NLRB sets rules aimed at keeping industry or labor from trampling employees' rights to organize themselves and it also protects the rights of employees to communicate freely with one another about work terms and conditions[66]. But even the National Labor Relations Board would appear to be unclear on the legalities of this controversial issue.

The legalities of technological workplace issues must be resolved as more and more cases of workplace discrimination and workplace invasion of privacy surface.

However, the ethical concerns remain. If employers and insurance companies have the genetic information available, is it ethical to discriminate in order to save the companies potential thousands of dollars? Is electronic snooping only a necessity due to legal concerns or is electronic snooping a substitution for poor leadership? If you work for a company at home, should they monitor your home equipment? Another issue at the forefront of workplace technological issues is the workplace literacy alerts and this will be discussed in the next section.

Part 2: Institutional and Societal Techno-Communication

- ➢ The Growing Divide

- ➢ Technological Literacy
  - o Workplace
  - o Communication Through Technology
  - o The Demise of Written and Nonverbal Communication
    - Grammar and E-mail
    - Miscommunication
    - Talking Computers

- ➢ Distance Learning: Educated Choices or Educational Technoism?

- ➢ Society and Technology: Fundamental yet Subtle Changes
  - o Technological Snooping
  - o The Internet: There is no Privacy so get Used to It

The Growing Divide

Global communication systems, interconnectedness, globally wired technology, knowledge economy, and twenty-first century information economy are just a few of the descriptors one might find in the technologically-controlled world we all live in today. We stand on a precipice, stepping into a new era, a time of enormous change and uncertainty characterized by the emergence of the first truly borderless, interconnected global economy[81]. Robert Rosen, in his book *Global Literacies,* explains:

> "Ours is a unique place in history. Not since the Industrial
> Revolution have we faced such forces in two fundamental
> areas of world society: the electronic information revolution
> and global economic interdependence. This isn't just a change
> of degree, but a fundamental change in kind. Globilization
> involves the integration of markets and nation-states enabling
> individuals, corporations, and countries to reach the world
> farther, faster, deeper, and cheaper. We live in a networked,
> interconnected world with computer devices embedded in
> telephones, cars, televisions, and household appliances. The
> Internet and electronic commerce are dramatically changing
> how we do business."

Juan Enriquez, in the book, *As the Future Catches You,* had it right when he said the digital revolution transformed not just computer companies but also television, cable, pagers, radio, newspapers, magazines, telephones and photography. Enriquez said that it did so by creating and spreading a new language and language is a powerful medium. "The digital alphabet encodes and transmits information with extraordinary speed and accuracy and it has become the world's main language," he said. With computers and the Internet dominating communications, a new language complete with jargons and slang has emerged. In fact, recently the Oxford English Dictionary added some of this high-tech language to the newer editions. Of these new words, this dictionary defined digital divide as "the gulf between those who have ready access to computers and the Internet and those who do not." This digital divide is a disturbing trend and has been predicted to worsen as the divide between the "haves" and the "have-nots" widens with the rapid development of new technologies. A recent *Reuters* study warned of the gap between those in the United States who participate in the growing on-line society and the mostly poor and elderly who do not is entrenched and unlikely to disappear soon.[9] This Consumer Federation of America study found that the gap between the Internet-connected and the disconnected in America is leaving millions lagging in key areas such as economic and civic activities as more services migrate to the Internet. A recent special report by a 2000 edition of *Futurist* listed fifty paths to success in the technologically driven 21st century calling it the "Opportunity Century." Some of the listings included, becoming a worker of the world, building wealth, getting rich, shopping anytime, anywhere, going global, getting involved virtually, living better through nanotechnology, and exploring the universe. All of these opportunities are possible through technology but threaten to leave the "have-nots" in the dust with little chance of using technology to become rich, shop anytime, build wealth or become a worker of the world. Charles

Handy, leading author, once said, "The most likely outcome of the knowledge era is an increasingly divided society unless we take urgent steps to distribute knowledge and intelligence more widely"[64].

A recent survey by *American Demographics* explained being tech-savvy isn't just about computer knowledge. This study found that today's tech-infused world has created gaps between the "tech-adept" and the "techno-twits" that are increasingly widening. Our homes and our offices demand our technological knowledge and will increasingly challenge us to obtain the newest, mainstream, super-fast broadband Internet to survive. This survey showed most people (82%) can fully operate their televisions and 60% of respondents could program their VCR's with no problem. Of course this tells us that in the year 2003, 18% of those surveyed still haven't figured out how their televisions fully operate and an astonishing 40% of those surveyed still have problems programming VCRs! The responses on home computer usage showed more than half, 56%, is less than certain how to fully operate their computer. The same percentage, 56%, admitted they were less than certain how to completely operate their cell phone. The tech-savvy or the "early adopters" in marketing lingo, are jumping ahead of society in largely proportional bounds, leaving the working class further and further behind. One attribute of the digital divide, technological language barriers, is threatening to dig the technologically challenged even deeper in a hole. The average person is unable to communicate in the technological jargon that is used by the upper echelon of technological circles. Many find it difficult to communicate even in the simplest of technological terms.

One recent study specifically focused on the digital divide finding 23.5% of black households and 23.6% of Hispanic households had Internet access while the rate in white households was 46.1%[19]. This study showed that there is a major gap between whites and people living in cities being more likely to have computers and Internet access than minorities or those living in rural areas. There is a gap when looking at the poor and the elderly and their participation in the technology-based society. Of the 1900 people polled in the aforementioned *Reuters* study, it was found that 47% did not have Internet access at their home, and half of those "disconnected" respondents did not own a computer. According to this study, almost two-thirds of the disconnected population expressed concern that technological progress could widen the gap between the rich and the poor. Author C. Taylor, in a recent *Time* magazine cautioned the phrase "digital divide" has become mired in the blurry realm of cliché, applied variously to women, the disabled, seniors, ethnic minorities, and rural and inner-city populations. This author described the digital divide well:

"Technology has moved so fast that a new upper-class-composed largely of the same white affluent, college-educated males that made up the old upper class-has spurted ahead of the rest of society, mostly because they have the time and money necessary to acquire and understand the tools of the digital revolution. This is not merely an apocalyptic vision. Members of this digital class are already banking and trading stocks over high-speed Internet connections and whipping out wireless Palm Pilots while others wait in sluggish teller lines with pockets full of Post-it notes. Buy on-line and you generally avoid sales tax; if shopping in the real world, your only option is, you pay the full whack. By 2004 there will also be a digital divide between 29 million households with super-fast broadband Internet access and the on-line equivalent of the middle class-those who still lumber along on 56K modems. Taken all together, these tiny day-to-day advantages potentially add up to a class gap of Dickensian proportions."

The significant proportional "class gap" the author referred to is leaving the working class behind, sometimes seen in the simplest component; communications. As most research has shown us, the elderly and the poor are being left behind in the technological showdown. The question remaining to be answered is how is the working class as a whole surviving? In an attempt to provide some answers to the questions, 100 surveys were distributed with 68 working class individuals responding.

The survey was conducted to determine if there is a technological language barrier. The surveyed were workers in industry, secretaries, human resource employees, retired individuals and participants still in school. The respondents were Hispanic, black and white and varied in age, gender, and educational level (see Table 1 for further information). The survey asked for translation of technological jargon and acronyms used and generally understood by the "haves" in technological circles. Some of this jargon and acronyms used by technological trendsetters has indeed made the cut in the Oxford Dictionary's latest revision. As stated previously, this survey was conducted to determine if the average person is being left behind in the knowledge society by the simplest element of communication, the simple word or acronym. The prediction was that very

few "everyday" working class people would be able to understand the simplest of

technological jargon. The survey deliberately included simple terms that most owners of

personal computers would recognize without a thought. This was to eliminate any

assumptions on levels of technological savvy. The survey asked that the respondents not

guess, ask others, or research the items but answer with "either you know or you don't"

response. Table 2 shows the results of the survey and Table 3 shows the correct responses

for each definition.

Table 1: Survey Respondents

100 Surveys	68% Response Rate
Average Age	40
Median Age	39
Youngest	11
Oldest	82
Std. Dev.	14.8
High School Graduates	46%
Some College	29%
College Graduate	18%

Table 2: Respondent Responses

Term	Correct Responses	Incorrect Responses
URL	18%	82%
Upload	35%	65%
MP3	38%	62%
Spamming	26%	74%
Snail Mail	51%	49%
Internet	78%	22%
i-Mode	0	100%
Icon	79%	21%
Hacker	82%	18%
Homepage	74%	26%
AOL	93%	7%
Gopher	13%	87%
IRC	4%	96%
WWW	81%	19%

Table 3: Correct Definitions

URL	Uniform Resource Locator or Web address
Upload	Move a file from your computer to another computer via modem
MP3	Music file exchange system
Spamming	Sending hundreds of same message to discussion groups
Snail Mail	U.S. Postal Service
Internet	Worldwide network linking computers
i-Mode	Japan's wireless Internet system
Icon	Small symbol displayed on computer screen to access programs or files
Hacker	Traditionally an avid user of computers but in Internet it refers to any traveler on the net
Homepage	First page of a website or document; e-front door
AOL	America On-Line
Gopher	A computer program that searches the net for subjects you specify. It scours and fetches Internet information
IRC	Internet Relay Chat: Real time
www	world wide web

One 30-year old respondent added a note to the survey explaining that he/she had only used a computer once. This person knew WWW and AOL and identified an icon as "the square you put your arrow on." This person, a high school graduate, also identified a hacker and the term upload correctly. Several others remarked that they felt "stupid" with the inability to fill in most of the answers. The study confirms the average working class person has very little computer experience. Some are aware of the most commonly used terms such as AOL and www that have become so common in the world today they have been added to the dictionary. Only 12 % of the respondents were over 60 years of age. However, the surveys were alarming and suggest we are indeed leaving our senior citizens behind in the technological revolution. 75% of these participants correctly identified AOL while 50% understood the term Internet. None of those over 60 years of age could define URL, Upload, MP3, or SPAMMING. Only one of those could define Icon and two individuals over 60 knew the definition of Hacker while three knew what www and Homepage meant. Only 10% of the survey respondents were 24 and under. But of those who did respond, 100% knew the definition of Internet, Hacker, Homepage, www, and AOL. 86% correctly recognized MP3, Snailmail, and Icon. The younger respondents did not recognize Japan's Internet system as i-Mode and only 14% knew the definition of Gopher, URL, and IRC. Of all 68 respondents, 100% could not correctly identify i-Mode as the Japanese Internet system. 96% could not identify IRC and 87% could not correctly identify gopher as a search program. However, 93% could identify AOL as America On-Line most likely due to brilliant advertising. Hacker was correctly identified on 82% of the surveys due to highly publicized cases of hackers destroying computer files. The true definition of Hacker is anyone who travels on the web but it has become the term describing illegal and unethical behavior. Overall, the survey results show us the working class is lagging further and further behind in technological knowledge. Even some correctly identifying such terms as AOL, Internet, and www admitted they had never used them but knew what they were. The results raise a red flag and should cause us to pause and reflect on the working class digital divide. As Paul Fussell noted in his book, *Class: A Guide Through the American Status System*, although there is tremendous confusion on how many "classes" we would find when breaking down the American status system, a full 80% of our population describe their own status as "middle class." If this statistic is accurate, the digital divide is only benefiting 20% of our population and the backbone of America, the working class, is lagging further and further behind. As we will discuss later, the workplace is changing and threatening the U.S. working class socio-economic status as well.

As suggested previously, the technological or on-line equivalent of the middle class could be already emerging. Juan Enriquez, in his book *As the Future Catches You*, reported that during a period of unprecedented growth and technological leadership, middle class bankruptcies increased from 313,000 in 1980 to 1,281,000 in 1999. This author found that two-thirds of these were people who had lost their jobs and found it impossible to catch up with a rapidly changing economy. With many manufacturing jobs relocating elsewhere, job loss is at an all time high and many of the unemployed admit to having no or less than adequate technological skills. When discussing the digital divide, it may be helpful to look at the study of Semiotics or the study of hidden American cultural systems signs and codes. Jack Solomon described the semiotic category of status in our culture[86]:

"American companies manufacture status symbols because American consumers want them. As Alexis Tocqueville recognized a century and a half ago, the competitive nature of democratic societies breeds a desire for social distinction, a yearning to rise above the crowd. But given the fact that those who do make it to the top in socially mobile societies have often risen from the lower ranks, they still look like everyone else. In the socially immobile societies of aristocratic Europe, generations of fixed social conditions produced subtle class signals. The accent of one's voice, the shape of one's nose, or even the set of one's chin, immediately communicated social status. Therefore, the demand for status symbols in America, for the objects that mark off social success, is particularly strong in democratic societies, where the aristocrat so often looks and sounds different from everyone else. Status symbols, then, are signs that identify the possessors' place in social hierarchy, markers of rank and prestige. But how do we know that something is a status symbol? The explanation is quite simple: when an object either costs a lot of money or requires influential connections to possess, anyone who possesses it must also possess the necessary means and influence to acquire it. The object itself really doesn't matter, since it ultimately

disappears behind the presumed social potency of its owner.

Semiotically, what matters is the signal it sends, its value as a sign

of power."

It can easily be seen through this study that the new status symbol or the new

dividing line is the digital divide. The line that separates the techno-savvy from the rest of

the society is widening and deepening with each new technological wonder. Clearly, the

survey shows most people are still struggling to understand the basic e-mail message

lingo. Harvard economist, Robert Reich wrote that "America is cleaving into symbolic

analysts and everyone else; the 20 percent would live lives of ease and wealth and

complete their secession from the union in guarded suburban enclaves while the poorest

Americans will be isolated within their own enclaves of urban and rural desperation and

the middle class gradually growing poorer, will feel powerless to alter any of these

trends."[64]

Recently, Walter Mossberg, author of the personal technology column for the

Wall Street Journal, discussed his 10th anniversary with this column and how technology

had changed since 1991. Although he noted unprecedented change in technological

advancements, he also noted that amazingly, some interesting things haven't changed:

- The techie class that designs and sells these products still tend to make them too
  complicated and still looks down on average consumers, at least privately

- The buying experience is still terrible

- While the PC has gotten easier, newer technologies, such as wireless home networking, are as depressingly complicated as computers once were

The last ten years has certainly seen unparalleled progress clearly demonstrated in Mossberg's experience. Jack Solomon's discussion on Semiotics and status explained to us that Americans look to status symbols to mark off social success and identify the possessors' place in social hierarchy and semiotically, what matters is the signal status objects sends, its value and its sign of power. Remember the 2000 *Reuters* study concluded that the gap between those in the United States who participate in the growing online society and the poor and the elderly who do not is entrenched and unlikely to disappear soon (after ten years, this hasn't changed much). In this study, of the 1900 people polled 47% did not have Internet access at their home, and half of those "disconnected" respondents did not own a computer. And in the year 2000, nearly ten years after Mossberg started his column, almost two-thirds of the disconnected population expressed concern that technological progress could widen the gap between the rich and the poor. The disconnected, even those who correctly define AOL and www, will be unable to participate in the computer culture. For example, several of the respondents remarked they had hardly touched a computer and they still knew the basic definitions of AOL and WWW and the Internet. Societal functioning is the ultimate test and many of our citizens are failing to function technologically in our society today.

Jargon and slang is typically utilized to purposely separate and isolate. One only has to look as far as teenagers to see the lengths they will go to separate and isolate themselves from adults. The instant messaging language used by so many today is used to send short text messages to others via the cell phone. "More and more teenagers are buying into the idea of communicating silently. They want private conversations," said Harry Martin, director of data sales for Verizon Wireless[56]. Teenagers and the purposeful communication glitches are not a major concern as historically teenagers will find whatever means to separate from parents. However, when jargon and slang are used to separate and isolate our working class citizens, it will play a role in how effective America will be as a player in the global market.

Even the workplace has changed drastically affecting the working class and their ability to function in an ever increasingly technical workplace. The workplace needs to be effective and efficient, involving employees in quality control and decision-making. If a large portion of the workforce is "workplace illiterate" businesses and industries will suffer in productivity. So with that said, what is considered "literate" today in the workplace? The upcoming section discusses the evolving workplace and how the technological literacy standards have drastically changed.

Technological Literacy

The Workplace

As many futurists have warned, the world is changing in ways that demand and reward greater knowledge and skills. The global economy, the Internet, NAFTA, and other developments have changed what it means to be literate[52]. Scholars, educators, and policymakers are all struggling with how to redefine literacy to reflect changes in society, a global economy, higher educational standards for all students, and advances in technology[49]. In 1991, the National Literacy Act on funding for workplace literacy programs offered a definition that is frequently considered standard:

> Literacy means an individual's ability to read, write, and speak in English,
> and compute and solve problems at levels of proficiency necessary to function
> on the job and in society, to achieve one's goals, and one's knowledge
> and potential.

This definition was a far cry from times past when literacy was considered the ability to read and write at a very basic level. In 1993, researchers observed that the current but evolving definition of what it means to be literate goes beyond the basic skills of reading and writing, and arithmetic[49]. Many researches have suggested that what has changed is not educational attainment, but the more sophisticated, technological demands of the workplace[49, 52, 44]. These researchers have blamed workplace illiteracy on the changing workplace practices and related demand for technical training and this is elevating the basic skills needed for many jobs. As technological advances continue to change the way we communicate, interact, get information, and do our jobs, a "literacy inflation" occurs. This doesn't necessarily mean Americans are becoming less literate over time but we raise the bar on literacy standards we expect them to achieve. Today's workplace requires other important skills such as higher order thinking and problem-solving skills, computer and other technology-related skills, and literacy skills in the context of the workplace[52]. In Northern Indiana, the Northern Indiana Workforce Investment Board recently shared a State of the Workforce Report: "While employers seek workers with traditional skills in areas like communications, basic math, problem-solving, listening and attention to detail, a growing number require workers who can use increasingly sophisticated technology." The employees in this representative sample shared that they needed workers who can use a computer and "this is threatening to guys who have been tightening nuts and bolts." This report noted a conflict in that while computer literate employees are important to employees, more than half the households in the region do not have computers at home. Even fewer - 38-40% - have Internet access. The Northern Indiana study could serve as a representative sample echoing a common concern of employers across our nation.

There is a positive correlation when comparing literacy levels and socio-economic statistics in our society[52]. 43% of people with the lowest literacy skills live in poverty, 17% receive food stamps, and 70% have no job or a part-time job. In addition, there is a growing and major gap between high paying, high-tech jobs and low paying service jobs in our society. And, the *Futurist* recently reported in the 21st century, the majority of

employees hired by manufacturers will be college graduates or will have job-specific,
post-high school training. Employees will need to possess the skills to program and
operate high-tech tools such as robots. The traditional blue-collar worker with only a
high-school diploma will sometimes be squeezed out and the majority of less-educated
former factory workers will take lower-paying jobs in the service sector. This has played
out in North Carolina where the textile industry, the lifeline for many workers, has
tragically died a slow death. Over the past five years in the Carolinas, scores of rumbling
mills have gone silent; 80,000 textile employees thrown out of work as globilization has
had an impact[93]. Of these jobless textile workers, 2/3 of those who found other jobs had
taken a cut in pay. The average age of the laid off mill worker is 43 and because it is
likely they will never adapt to fit emerging jobs, their future looks bleak. One 61 year old
laid-off mill worker worried that the country is becoming a country of services and those
jobs don't pay as much. This is indeed a disturbing trend that threatens America's
working class. The *Wall Street Journal* warned if only the wealthy can afford computers
and computers become essential to the success of any business then the prospects for the
underprivileged will only diminish[64].

The inflation on workplace literacy definition and the downward spiral of the poor
and working class serves as a small-scale model of society and warns us of things to
come. When Technoism, or suppressed skepticism, causes American citizens to turn their
head and ignore the obvious warnings, we allow the digital divide to flourish. Technoism
causes us to ignore the working class and their downward spiral in their socio-economic

status. Even working class members fall victim to Technoism, silenced by their fears of being left behind.

There have been some recent reports and theories proposing the digital divide is only fiction and does not really exist, but statistics tell a different story. It is obvious the "Techno-twits" and the Techno-lost will never gain ground and reach the status of the "Techno-savvy." Technological development benefits all of us and continues to better our lives in many ways; however, if technological success is saved for a few elite for the purpose of status and power, the whole of society suffers. Juan Enriquez offers a bigger picture clearly demonstrating the reason Technoism and the digital divide should be a major concern for our society:

> "...many countries just don't get it. They continue to invest primarily
> in stuff they can see and touch even though two-thirds of the global
> economy is already a knowledge economy. They do not invest in, or
> attract smart people who are science-literate. They do not get
> particularly concerned as many of their brightest leave. They forget you
> need even fewer people, time, or capital to build a nation, become a
> an economic superpower, wage war effectively, or launch a global
> business, but you do need technology-literate people. Lack of
> technology literacy is one of the reasons the gap between rich and the
> poorer countries in the world is growing so quickly....there is
> a 390:1 gap. The difference between what one person produces in

the richest and poorest countries in the world is no longer 5:1 but 390:1

and with IT and genetics, the difference will soon be more than

1000:1. The difference is that one educated individual can produce

a lot more. The consequences of ignoring technology or thinking

things can just go on are more severe than ever before."

We must all follow the lead of the new IBM president who took the reins in 1993.

He vowed to get rid of some of the language particular to that one company[28]. The first

thing he did was banish the IBMism LOB (Line of business). This IBM president surely

realized this "bluespeak" was isolating and sent a message of superiority rather than a

team and global mindset. In our society, a component of a "global mindset" is the

investment in educating all citizens in the communication required to operate in our

technologically-driven society. We can use IBM as a model in recognizing the need for a

common language. Just as we provide ESL (English as a Second Language) training to

our increasing Hispanic population, we must provide technological literacy training with

business and educational support and Governmental support through educational grants.

The recommendation that all citizens reach the same level of technological finesse is not

an achievable goal. There needs to be recognition of more than one class of technological

progression being possible. Therefore, an effort to support education of all citizens in the

basics of the technological language is an attainable goal. A clear definition of literacy

must be resolved for a comprehensive transfer of knowledge affording all citizens

equality in basic communication and inclusion into the technology revolution.

Communication Through Technology

Technological Communication is a topic that covers a multitude of issues such as workplace literacy in the workplace and the technological isolation of jargon and lingo. There are other communication issues attributed to technology. Whether cyber-apartheid, as Robert Putnam in the book, *Bowling Alone*, named the digital divide, miscommunications, or social isolation, our society finds digital communication to be a major issue facing our society today.

Robert Putnam noted challenges associated with computer-mediated communications in our society. He quoted Sociologist Manuel Castells:

"…..because access to computer-mediated communication is culturally, educationally, and economically restrictive, and will be so for a long time, the most important cultural impact of computer-mediated communication could be potentially the reinforcement of the culturally dominant social networks."

A second issue Putnam addressed is the fact that digital communications does not include nonverbal communications and the subtle clues this provides in interpersonal relationships and interactions. He suggested its possible nonverbal communication offered significant survival advantage during the long course of human evolution. Putnam quoted organizational theorists Nitin Nohria and Robert Eccles who pointed out face-to-face encounters provide a depth and speed of feedback that is impossible in computer-mediated communication. These theorists believe that increased computer-mediated communication will actually require more frequent face-to-face encounters: "an extensive, deep, robust social infrastructure of relationships must exist so that those using the electronic media will truly understand what others are communicating to them. When you overlay an electronic community directly on top of a physical community, this creates a very powerful social pressure to be civil. If you are going to yell at someone on the Net, or flame them out, you may run into them at the grocery store, and they may turn out to be your neighbor." In other words, Putnam added, social capital may turn out to be a prerequisite for, rather than a consequence of, effective computer-mediated communication.

Seth Godin, in a 2001 *Fast Company* article, agreed. He asked, "Have you noticed that people you know are far less likely to cut you off in traffic, curse at you, or steal your parking space than total strangers seem to be? There's a reason: Anonymity is the enemy of civility." Godin warned that given total privacy and a cloak of invisibility, many people become coarse. They do selfish things-things they would never do if a friend or video camera were watching. Godin argued all the warnings that we are entering an era of Big Brother are wrong-it is an era of anonymity. In some cases technological anonymity has been beneficial, however. When officers of the law track on-line predators of adolescents, the anonymity allows for officers to pose as adolescents to track the on-line seducers of children. But anonymity will be abused in many cases and Godin listed those who benefit from on-line anonymity[41]:

1. Online auction services which could lead to fraud and fraudulent bidding.

2. Anonymous SPAM mail clogging our inboxes would disappear if the messages could be traced or a bill sent out for those costs.

3. Information exchange is crippled as a result of anonymous rumors and untruths. After a time no one knows who said what.

Grammar and E-mail

Godin described a workplace where everyone wears a mask referring to what e-mailing has done to the workplace today. And to add insult to injury, the cyber communication so prevalent in the workplace today may contain grammar and writing errors that would not have been tolerated in business communications in the past. Shannon McGuire, an English instructor at Louisiana State University has noticed an increasing indifference toward the rules of grammar, spelling, and sentence structure[31]. McGuire has had students say to her that their future employers will not care about semicolons, commas, and "stuff like that." McGuire blames slack writing habits on E-mail, Instant Messaging, and our casual society.

Addicted to Digital Communication

Slack writing habits, of course, are major communication issues, but an even more disturbing communication issue is the societal isolation resulting from on-line addictions. A recent Stanford study examined over 4000 adults in its attempt to assess the

social consequences of Internet use. About two-thirds of those surveyed reported

spending fewer than five hours per week on the Net and these "light" users reported few

life changes. However, the other third of "regular" users, who spent more than five hours

per week online, reported significant life changes. Of these, the "heavy" users-the 15% of

the total who surpassed ten hours per week-reported the largest life changes. Principle

investigator Norman Nie warned that the more time people spend on the Internet, the less

time they spend with real human beings such as family and friends. He cautioned that we

need to monitor this trend carefully as a society[39]. Experts say several factors push some

people toward Web addiction. The Web lets some people escape from anxiety,

depression, or the pain of relationships said Dr. Kimberly Young, executive director of

the Center for Online Addiction in Bradford, IL[95]. A person who is a failure in life can

connect in Chat rooms. This behavior is the most damaging thing Web addiction does as

it keeps people from connecting with real people and family[95]. Dr. Jonathan Kandell,

director of counseling services at the University of Maryland, College Park commented

that people become expert when dealing with others online, but have difficulty talking to

people face-to-face[95]. If we are honest, we know we all have made a phone call and

prayed to get the person's voice mail for fear of actually getting into a real conversation

with another human being. Indeed, that would be much too time consuming. And of

course, as previously discussed, many times this type of mechanistic and anonymous

communication allows for aggravated individuals to vent without thought towards others.

Miscommunication

Miscommunication attributed to technology has even affected the highest offices of the United States government. Since September 11, 2001, there has been finger-pointing and accusations flowing freely between government agencies. Could 9/11 have been prevented if agencies had shared information? The House and Senate investigations have revealed interesting revelations. Some of the failures are blamed on technology. The United States spends about $50 billion a year on computer systems, many of which are so incompatible that a piece of information can't travel from one system to another. There were also sensitivity issues whereas many officials lacked clearance to view sensitive information locked within certain agency's computer systems.

Talking Computers

In the future, will there be these types of communications problems? Of course not, say some futurists. Many futurists predict a future where there will be no writing at all while the computer will be our primary communication tool. William Crossman recently predicted the voice in/voice out computer will make literacy unnecessary by the year 2050. Talking computers, he reported in the December, 1999 issue of *The Futurist,* will make it possible for us to replace all written language with spoken language. We will be able to store and retrieve information simply by talking, listening, and looking at graphics, not at text. Crossman referred to written language as a technology, "a technological solution to specific information storage and retrieval problems that people faced at a specific moment in history and like most technologies, written language will serve its function until some better technology comes along."[18] Written language, according to Crossman, is a transitory technology. The Trickster would have us believe written communication is only a stepping-stone to our technological future. This is a frightening prediction when considering the unknown potential technological failures. At the time, Y2K was a mystery and gave many individuals and businesses pause for concern. Although it proved to be a false alarm, what other unforeseen technological failures may be in our future? Will Technoism silence those who would challenge the demise of written communication?

Higher educational institutions are changing their communication modes as more and more students (customers) seek the convenience of technological education to achieve their degrees. Students demand technological or digital-educational opportunities demonstrating their preference to step away from the traditional classroom into a cyber-educational experience. The next section will discuss this evolving form of education.

Distance Learning: Educated Choices or Educational Technoism?

Many higher educational institutions encourage development and implementation

of on-line courses or distance learning. E. T. Robinson recently warned, "In the milieu of

technological change, the integration of distance education into any university may not

only appear to be the logical next step, but may even suggest the possibility of a financial

windfall."[71] According to market researcher, International Data Corporation, about two

million students take on-line courses from U.S higher educational institutions and that

number is predicted to elevate to five million by the year 2006[7]. This research also

observed that nearly one half of the 4000 major colleges and universities in the U.S. now

offer courses over the Internet or use the Web to enhance college classes. The questions

needing to be answered include; what are the long-term implications for faculty, what is

the quality of student learning, and are courses offered using appropriate learning

environments? Is Technoism the driving force behind the inundation of technology in

educational institutions and will faculty be allowed to make educated choices without

fear of reprisal?

Recently *Chronicle of Higher Education* shared the results of a survey on distance

learning. It was found that attitudes toward distance education were more favorable

among those who had taught distance-learning courses. In fact, 72% of this cohort felt

positive about distance learning. In addition, 51% of faculty members who had not taught

distance classes felt positive about distance learning[10]. However, of those 72% who had

tried distance learning, there was a general apprehension about the faculty time

commitment and increased workloads encouraged by higher educational institutions.

Faculty is not typically paid more for on-line courses and the development and time commitment expected is significantly higher than the time spent in traditional preparation and classroom teaching. In addition, faculty members at numerous colleges and universities have expressed concern of forced participation in distance learning development and facilitation of e-courses[89]. Will Technoism allow academic institutions to take the power and control for curriculum decisions from faculty? In fact, in 1996 the American Federation of Teachers released a paper on the use of technology in education encouraging faculty members to seek curbs on the adoption of technology in teaching[90]. The Federation also encouraged faculty members to utilize technology in teaching while encouraging opposition to courses taught on the Internet unless it meets faculty members' standards of quality. Most importantly, the paper encouraged the bargaining for employment contracts that protect the jobs of faculty members who choose *not* to use the new technologies. For fear that non-compliance will jeopardize jobs; Technoism silences the faculty who question the overuse of technology in education.

Overall research shows there is meager criticism from faculty members on the inundation of distance learning into higher education. But critics who have spoken out question the increased workloads and lack of increased salary for the extra workload. There is also widespread concern about forced use of new technologies in classrooms and the fate of those who choose the traditional route in education[89]. The few outspoken have also warned about the possible loss of power of curriculum in academe. Without a doubt, distance learning has a place in higher education. However, we must not allow

Technoism to silence the critics. Faculty members should be allowed to make educated
choices without fear of retribution.

Another faculty concern focuses on the quality of educational learning provided
to students. Recently, faculty at Washington State University objected to an initiative
involving courses to be delivered solely on the Internet and via e-mail because it was
feared faculty would "enable learning without any direct contact with faculty."[40] At the
elite Harvard Business School, there is a general belief it would be impossible to replicate
its classroom education online[7]. Similarly, last year MIT faculty nixed teaching classes
online fearing it would detract from the residential experience. MIT does post classroom
notes and syllabi, but that is no substitute for actual teaching so faculty is not worried
about the threat to classroom learning. Barry Munitz, past Chancellor of the California
State University System and current president and chief executive officer of the J. Paul
Getty Trust suggests, "Ironically, the greatest challenge (of the convenience institutions)
will be to our most respected institutions, for they are least likely to perceive a threat or to
feel any need to challenge their basic assumptions."[74] Mr. Munitz continued by
suggesting Ivy League institutions couple the perception of quality with restricted access
to it. He envisioned a world where students could choose between an Ivy League
education and a canned convenience program through on-line courses. Mr. Munitz
paused to question the quality-price association. Ivy League Schools have indeed taken
the high road. But in other cases, Technoism dictates decision-making even when on-line
education produces less than desirable results. Recently Byron Brown, a Michigan State
University economics professor, researched how on-line students measured up to

classroom students, both taking the same economics course[74]. His findings, published in the *American Economic Review*, show that virtual students generally scored significantly lower on examinations than did classroom students, especially when attempting more complex problems[63]. Yes, on-line courses are financially beneficial for educational institutions, but is it providing a proper educational experience for students? In 2000, Peter Manicas stated in the paper, *Higher Education on the Brink:*

> "The traditional university is highly labor intensive and thus costly. Currently, except in the convenience institutions, the use of technologies have tended to supplement, rather than replace older modes and thus have added to costs without much gain. As always, technology has both a light side and a dark side. The dark side is likely to become the one realized. Thus, instead of improved discussion, equality of discussion among all members, collaborative and active learning, the instructor as expert and facilitator, we are getting taped lectures, canned WEB courses, automated correspondence courses, and more generally, a minimizing of high-cost active instruction for low-cost automation."

Even K-12 educators have questioned the benefits of technology in the classroom. There is a growing concern that there is too much emphasis on technology in classrooms; that schools are throwing money at it and not getting much in return[85]. "There is no evidence that using computers or the Internet improves learning," said Alan Warhaftig, coordinator of Learning in the Real World."[85] Technoism seems to be driving K-12 as observed through the following statement by Hank Bromley, professor of education at

State University of New York at Buffalo: "Schools, pushing for technology in the classroom, need to ask themselves whether it fits in with some educational vision. Too often, administrators go to the latest technology because of some nebulous sense that they will be left behind if they don't. First they get it and then they try to figure out what to do with it."[85] The Trickster fools us into believing we need it, Technoism silences those who question it, and as a result schools invest our dollars on technological equipment that may never be used in a classroom. As an educator, I experienced Technoism in the most expensive way a couple of years ago. I wanted a projector in my classroom for displaying slides. I observed the textbook instructor materials came with a CD-Rom and I reasoned I must have the technological equipment for a techno-classroom. The budget did not allow for the purchase of a projector at that time. I purchased a $3000 projector out of my own pocket, convinced I could use it when I did outside speaking engagements as well. I looked forward to the beginning of the fall semester. But after about three weeks of class, I reflected and realized the use of the projector and canned CD-Rom led me to "lecture." I typically plan for my classroom to be interactive and collaborative. I arrange seating for open-discussion as I have never felt lecturing to be an effective method of teaching. I quit using the equipment immediately. I do have the equipment, however, and I suppose that makes me a part of the techno-savvy elite club.

We must not allow Technoism to flourish and silence those questioning the use of technology in education. Those who question may lead to elimination of ill-advised educational pursuits on the Internet. Those who question or challenge the "get on board" atmosphere of on-line course offerings, sometimes simply question the appropriateness of particular learning environments.

Controversies over distance learning are not debates between "Modernizers" and "Luddites" but disagreements over the particular situations in which distance learning is appropriate[89]. I recently opened a course catalog of a local higher educational institution and noticed a distance learning course on "Public Speaking." How does one develop appropriate speaking and presentation skills over the Internet? For example, one may be able to learn the control panel of aircraft, but would you fly with a pilot that took the course on-line and had no practical experience? Most likely not. I certainly dread the day when I open a course catalog from a university and see an on-line course for, "100 easy steps to brain surgery in eight weeks on-line." On-line courses certainly offer more flexible delivery. However, one question remains; how effective is the learning experience and what are the long-term implications for the students? Financially profitable for educational institutions; yes. Educationally responsible for students of educational institutions; not always. Margaret Stewart, in the March, 2001 *Teaching Professor*, shared her experience with distance learning. She stated, "I came away from even a positive experience of e-teaching feeling ambivalent. The time may come when disadvantages appear so inevitable that they become invisible as well. That time will certainly come if we do not highlight what we are perceiving now."[40] Professor Stewart expressed hope that by sharing conflicted feelings, we will share a constructive future for distance learning. As stated previously, the "ambivalence" seems to live through inappropriate uses of distance learning. Andy DePaolo, director of Stanford Center for

Professional Development commented recently that on-line instruction will never be as good as face-to-face instruction[7]. His center does, however, offer some on-line graduate courses in engineering. It is evident that most faculty are open-minded and willing to experiment with e-learning, however, there are reservations for potential abuse of the device allowing financial gains to rule over quality of education. Technoism, silencing those critics, quickens the acceleration of misuse of distance learning. When Technoism flourishes, courses such as "Public Speaking" will be offered on-line.

The partnering of education and technology will be part of educator's professional careers. "Get on board or be left behind," "It is the future of education," we are told as we are pushed and prodded towards distance learning adoption and acceptance. These types of admonishments which educators experience routinely are products of Technoism. It isn't that e-learning has no value. As one author stated, "Unless universities reclaim their core purpose-taking responsibility for higher education in the sense of higher order knowing, ability to synthesize and integrate the fragmented pieces of the meta-processes at work in society-the megatrends of dehumanization will become world destiny[4]." This author continues by proposing that what is needed is the courage of university leaders and faculty generally to reclaim their potentially powerful and central position of providing value-added knowledge-wisdom-not just bytes of information.

Technoism may be the driving force behind the questionable inundation of technology in educational institutions; however, there is no question the Internet is changing our perceptions of how educational environments should look. Educators need to step back, evaluate technology in our institutions and make educated choices without

fear of reprisal or condemnation.

Society and Technology: Fundamental yet Subtle Changes

Technological Snooping

Workplace monitoring systems are not the only privacy concern of citizens today. Most Americans say that even though they lack technology savvy, they know enough to believe that the Internet threatens their privacy and security[60]. Pew Internet and American Life Project conducted a survey in 2001 and found Americans are most concerned about on-line credit card thefts (87%), terrorist attacks (82%), large-scale fraud (80%), or hackers taking control of government computers (78%) and business hackers (76%).[60]Although a majority of citizens support new technologies enabling FBI and other agencies to monitor suspects' e-mail, many oppose such practices, fearing the technology could end up being used to read innocent people's messages. Surveillance has been at the forefront of many people's thoughts since news reports told us of the surveillance system at the 2001 Super Bowl which detected several people wanted by the law within the audience. This facial character recognition technology was developed by the Massachusetts Institute of Technology (MIT) and is a branch of biometrics[55]. Tampa Florida followed suit and is using high-security cameras in the party district, Ybor City. The cameras are linked to computer software that will scan crowds and using face-recognition systems, will match results to a database of wanted criminals. Other snooping technology has been utilized to spy on criminals. A whole new generation of surveillance technology has been developed that can see through clothing and peer into private homes[1]. Unfortunately, some of this technology is already turning up at airports, prisons, border crossings, and crime scenes. After September 11, 2001, we may all be shocked to find out when, where, and how we are being observed. The Supreme Court has not favored snooping technology and has insisted police get search warrants before being allowed to snoop into someone's private home. But with terrorist cells living amongst us, this is bound to change as well.

Global Positioning Systems can now be used to track a missing person to an area the size of a tennis court. The GPS uses signals from 24 satellites to identify direction, speed, and location of any object on Earth that has a GPS receiver. For security reasons, signals of civilian receivers in the past were "fogged," locating the receivers no more precisely than 300-600 feet. Now the government will stop "fogging" and the system will locate receivers within 30-60 feet. This system has other uses and is not only used to track criminals as the Facial Recognition Systems. In fact, parents are beginning to rely on the GPS systems to track their children. A child wearing a special watch or clip-on device can be tracked with the GPS system. For example, once the GPS gadget establishes its position, it then uses cell phone technology to send the information to the Internet where parents can log on and view a map of their child's location. Although this technology is most beneficial in a time of increased child abduction, as with most technology, there is the potential for abuse. Could we all be "tracked" eventually? Technology visionary, Jeff Wacker, thinks so. Mr. Wacker believes we will all be wearing computers soon[76]. He predicts that mobile technology and computing will go far beyond wireless handheld devices. He sees a future where everyone wears tiny computers that will monitor their health, help them work smarter, and enrich their lives. In fact, Mr. Wacker owns a computer ring he wears and it acts as a digital identification card, a smart card, a homing beacon, and a data-encryption machine. Could it be much longer before we all wear GPS computers or devices implanted in our wearable computers that utilize the facial recognition system? In July 2001, a man rented a minivan from a Rent-a-car company in New Haven, Connecticut only to find out later it had a global positioning system implanted in the vehicle. The device recorded him speeding in three states and each incident, digitally recorded, added a $150 charge to his rental bill. And if we haven't already had enough digitalized advertising, it is predicted that soon your wireless phone service will be able to track you so advertisers can share specialized advertising for specific locations. The reasoning for this annoyance upgrade is a Federal Communications Commission regulation requiring providers of wireless phone service to be able to report the location of a 911 caller. It makes it possible for carriers to pinpoint the location of a wireless caller within 50 yards.

The Trickster mixes things up again as innovation and protective services are used as a means for invasion of privacy and intrusion into our lives. The Facial Recognition System and X-ray vision device is meant to save us from the dangerous criminal but sets us up to be tracked and/or watched anytime, anyplace. GPS is a tool to protect our children but the technology opens up a world of intrusive possibilities. The ability to call 911 in emergencies offers hope in saving lives, however, it turns the wireless system against us as they track our whereabouts and sell the information to advertisers and SPAMMERS. Technoism rears its ugly head and silences the few critics of these devices making the alarmists powerless to change the technological threat to our American freedoms.

Could George Orwell's futuristic predictions where citizens would be under around the clock surveillance be coming reality? George Orwell may have predicted the Big Brother phenomenon; however, even George Orwell couldn't have foreseen the power and impact of the Internet.

The Internet: There is No Privacy so Get Used to It

No other technological achievement has raised privacy concerns as much as the Internet. No one has caused quite the stir about Internet privacy as Shaun Fanning. Shaun Fanning, in 1999, wrote the source code for the music file-sharing program called Napster[45]. Fanning combined the features of existing programs: the instant messaging system of Internet Relay Chat, the file-sharing functions of Microsoft Windows and the advanced searching and filtering capabilities of various search engines[45]. Napster has changed the world but not without stepping on a few toes along the way. The Recording Industry Association of America has sued Napster claiming the website and Fanning's program are facilitating the theft of intellectual property[45]. Attorneys for the recording industry are suing for tributary copyright infringement which means Fanning isn't accused of violating copyright but of contributing to and facilitating other people's infringement. And in a major setback to Napster, the Ninth Circuit Court of Appeals in San Francisco sided with the recording industry and ruled that Napster must stop helping its users exchange unauthorized, copyrighted material[15]. Fanning and his Napster only pioneered the way. Every industry that trades intellectual property-from publishing to needlework patterns-could get Napsterized[15]. What is the future of free music? It is really

a thing of the past as Napster and other on-line music services become fee-based. The

movie industry has stepped forward and is also asking for protection as more and more

DVD recordings are shared on the Internet. It is clear that we have and will continue to

have new and unexpected legal issues to address as we increase our digital dependencies.

Internet privacy can be a little more personal. Consumers who use the Internet to

shop, bank, or just visit websites of personal interest are feeling the sting of privacy

invasion. Personal information is vulnerable to abuse. The ability to establish a digital

trail is unlike anything we've had so far in history[3]. This means that e-businesses get high

prices for sharing personal consumer information. Hospitals and schools, for example, are

constructing vast national databases with everything "from your child's fourth grade

report card to the unique twists and turns of your DNA and businesses want that

information and in the online world, virtually every piece of data is for sale"[3].

Technology has made it possible for anyone in the world to know anything about us and

has made it possible for us to be available to anyone, anytime.

Lets look a little closer at how we lose our privacy every time we innocently

"surf" the web. Many unsuspecting individuals are unaware that every time they look at a

web page, "cookies," or mini computer files recording your surfing habits, gather

information about you while you are on-line. Every computer on the Internet is assigned

an IP (Internet Protocol) address allowing it to receive data[14]. Your web browser may give

away information about you and this information is available to anyone who wishes to access this personal list. This information is valuable to marketers and some web sites could actually sell your information to other marketers. I have a friend who recently posted her resume on a well-respected job search web page. She immediately began to get flooded with SPAM selling anything and everything. In a matter of minutes, her name was dispersed to every functioning marketer on the Internet. She received no job offers but had all the information she needed to lose weight, enlarge body parts, and re-finance her home.

A government-based web site should be the one place that is private but recently there was a warning that people who log onto dozens of federal government web sites could be tracked. Most people have moved some portion of their life to the web. Your personal numbers are most likely found somewhere on the net, and with the ingenuity usually found in thieves, your numbers are there for the asking. Many people today have reported identity theft and their stories are similar. Someone unbeknownst to you discovers your personal information and transfers money from your bank account or charges purchases on your credit card. Apparently, anyone with a checking account number and bank routing number can shift money electronically to another account. Unfortunately, these numbers are available at the bottom of your checks and easy to access electronically. The Federal Trade Commission gets about three thousand identity theft complaints and queries each week, up from four hundred a year ago[95].

The Federal Trade Commission has been paying attention to privacy concerns more and more as these complaints have increased. In 1998, the FTC conducted a survey of web sites and found that 92% collected information[33]. Of those web sites, only 14% provided any notice about privacy practices. Despite the concern, any federal bills that have been introduced are still pending.

With all the government protections delayed, hackers have been having their way with our personal and business computer systems. According to watchers of malicious codes, hacking is becoming a national past-time for computer enthusiasts tempted to test their skills against the establishment[96]. Since 1998, the number of hacking attacks and virus releases has increased sevenfold. Viruses are being produced at a rate of a dozen or more a day with some causing tens of millions of dollars in damage and lost productivity[96]. Hackers trick unsuspecting e-mailers into replying to tricky messages and some of these viruses are intended to infect the person's computer and possible every e-mail address in that person's address book. And without governmental interventions and legislative protection, many web sites you enter could be false fronts. Hackers, involved in web site spoofing, can mimic the home page of a legitimate web site so to gather personal information on customers.

Our Government is whom we look to for protection and yet we find examples of governmental sharing of citizen's private information. Governments around the country have been attempting to put records on-line and some of this information can be personal. In some cases, a person's divorce records, bankruptcy records, arrest records, and traffic violations records can be accessed[14]. If you live in Ohio, anyone who types your name in a database can find out how much your home is worth, the floor plans, and placement of your windows and doors[14]. Critics have a name for this on-line process: a breaking and entering handbook[14].

The Internet is quickly becoming the center of our lives. For example, innovators are experimenting with Internet long distance calls. All our services could soon be provided via Internet in the future. Today a person can even arrange virtual visits with their doctors on-line. In fact, a pilot program has been tested in Silicon Valley and if the web visits are a success, some HMO's may pay for on-line visits in the near future. Of course, E-health will be another personal open-book for all to see.

Scott McNealy, CEO of Sun Microsystems, one of the world's largest Internet companies, once said, "You already have zero privacy, so get over it." With GPS, FRS, X-ray snooping devices, hackers, and sharing and selling of personal information over the net, it may be that Mr. McNealy was right on with this frightening but factual statement.

AT THE CROSSROADS: TECHNOLOGICAL ASSESSMENT AND ANALYSIS

- ➤ Societal Assessment

    - o Office of Technology Assessment (OTA)
    - o Technological Immersion

- ➤ Organizational Assessment
    - o Business and Industry
    - o Educational Institutions

- ➤ Individual Assessment

At the Crossroads: Technology Assessment and Analysis

The Trickster and his friend Technoism will only be a memory when there is
opportunity for educated assessment of technology without fear of reprisal. Technology
and Society are at a crossroads. At this crossroads is an opportunity to make the changes
and turnaround needed for a positive journey into the future. Technology development
will continue to benefit our lives in ways we can only imagine. Technology can be used
as a tool to improve our environment, save lives through disease detection, and to connect
us globally. It can be used to improve relationships, educate from a distance, and make
multi-party corporate and governmental decisions. The technological contributions to our
society are astounding and miraculous, however, these very tools can be used to exploit,
discriminate, and to destroy. There is a gap in the technology development and utilization
process and that gap is the much needed steps of assessment and analysis. There are three
levels of assessment and analysis beginning with societal technological impacts.
Secondly, organizations need to consider assessments and analysis before jumping on
board to buy the latest and greatest technology. And lastly, there needs to be assessment
at the individual level. How far do we go before we step back and assess the impact
technology has in our personal and work lives?

Societal Assessment

Office of Technology Assessment (OTA)

In 1972, there was a considerable debate over the best technique to assess technology. Congress introduced a bill that would create an Office of Technology Assessment (OTA). There were concerns, of course. Would an OTA office derail technological development and creativity? In 1972, business leaders from companies such as Motorola, GE, Bell Labs, and Rockwell Corporation expressed concern. Outside Congress, there was a growing skepticism that any formal organization could properly evaluate the impact of technological change on the environment, the economy, and society (www.wws.princeton.edu/~ota/ns20/ota72_n.html). Some of the quotes offered on this web page were:

1. Daniel Noble, retired vice chairman of Motorola and head of the company's Science Advisory Boards: "If such an office is expected to anticipate the impact of science and engineering over the long term, this is absurd."

2. William Baker, vice-president for research and patents at Bell Labs: "I don't know where you'd start in the course of innovation to make technology assessments…you could only be sure to restrain technical progress."

3. Arthur Bueche, General Electric's vice-president for research and development, said he wouldn't mind an office functioning as an

"information activity for members of Congress." But he warned that if the OTA were to be set up as "a police activity" it would stifle innovation.

The formation of OTA seems visionary and revolutionary as it would have been difficult for anyone to foresee the exponential progress of the technology revolution. Vary Coates, a project director and senior associate at OTA from 1984-1995, shared some personal reflections during an e-mail communication. She noted OTA did not really do technology assessment in the full sense of impact assessment, but it did do excellent objective policy analysis studies on issues arising from technology. OTA was eliminated in 1995, a victim of congressional cuts. Dr. Coates reported OTA did not act as "an early warning system" for the Congress as originally envisioned because they had to wait for the issues to be on the congressional radar screen in order to persuade committees to request a study. She explained that OTA methodology took time and was often out of step with the congressional calendars.

In the paper, *Technology Forecasting and Assessment in the United States: Statistics and Prospects*, Dr. Coates explained technology assessment[13]: "Technology assessment (TA) analyzes potential direct and indirect consequences of new or changing technology. It identifies possible impacts on the environment, the economy, social institutions and behaviors, and personal and collective quality of life." (p.5). She explained the role of legislators in the technology assessment movement: "Both corporate and government managers have become accustomed to utilizing forecasts of demographers, economists, meteorologists, and traffic engineers; but they are still slow to take into account the projectory of technological development and even more reluctant to anticipate its inevitable waves of societal impacts. This is especially true of legislators, who are generally unsophisticated about science and technology, are oriented toward reacting to problems rather than anticipating and avoiding them, and are leery of stepping ahead of daily preoccupations of their constituents."

Arnold Brown, Chairman of Weiner, Edrich, Brown, Inc., cautioned that we as a society should have a workable technology-assessment process that would effectively bridge the now gaping chasm between science/technology and policy[6]. In fact, in 2001 a workshop in Washington D.C. attended by a group of leading professional societies, universities, and think tanks met to discuss the issue of technological assessment. Technological assessment is of central importance to many practicing leaders in the United States. An interesting point is that fifteen European parliaments have now created technology analysis units and these units were inspired by the now defunct OTA. These leaders of the European organizations were reported to be dumbfounded when Congress voted to abolish the OTA in 1995. The Briefing Notes from this 2001 workshop noted that the leaders of these European organizations found it "incomprehensible" that the leading democratic legislature in the world should no longer have its own source of scientific and technical analysis.

Vary Coates predicted a new burst of interest in technology assessment. She listed some of the things that would make this likely:

➢ A series of technologically-driven disasters

> Growing resistance to more subtle societal or environmental impacts of technology, such as loss of privacy, structural unemployment, or an increasing income-education-health-housing gap between rich and poor Americans

> Awareness that social benefits have been sacrificed or opportunities missed because of regulatory indifference or corporate market-driven or profit-maximizing R & D strategies

> Evidence that TA-like institutions in other countries had helped to avoid, or at least called governments' attention to, such impacts

Dr. Coates predicted a new OTA might assess and forecast independently selected emerging technologies and technology-related issues for the dual purpose of sparking and informing public discussion and forewarning of potential impacts and issues.
The workshop held in Washington, D.C. in 2001 attempted to generate interest in creating a new form of OTA. Workshop participants repeatedly expressed the view that it is urgent that Congress take steps to obtain the strongest analytical support to inform its judgment on technology issues.

There is a need for the creation of a new type of office of assessment, similar but more encompassing than the original OTA. Trickster gains power when Technoism silences the critics, therefore an Office of Technology Assessment is the voice for the analysis and assessment of the technological impact on our society.

Technological Immersion

In 1998 Californians voted to replace bilingual education with an intensive English-immersion program aimed at getting students into regular classrooms. Arizonians followed this lead in 2000. There are other states considering this move. The English-immersion programs were developed so bilingual students would not be forced into special classrooms and would be allowed to join mainstream classrooms after the one-year English-immersion program. There are two reasons why voters proposed this option. One reason is the recognition of the growing Hispanic population in our schools today. Some of these students live in homes where English is not spoken and this presents a problem for educational institutions and the students when the students are unable to communicate in a mainstream classroom. Secondly, voters proposed this option because these students were lacking the basic communications skills required to succeed in school. These students were not provided the tools (English speaking) at home to function in the United States educational system.

The statistics have shown us that there are many students lacking the basic technological skills to succeed today. Children in homes without computers have huge disadvantages when compared to those students who do have the technology at home. And as more and more services and everyday functions migrate to the Internet, entire families are left behind as technology passes them by. Workers will lose jobs as they become more technologically complex. The blue-collar workers will be forced into service industry jobs as workplace literacy inflation makes it difficult for limited educated employees to survive. The elderly, many fearing the unknown, will continue to lag behind and soon will not even recognize the digital world that surrounds them.

The lack of awareness or the ignoring of the growing digital divide reminds us of the frog and the boiling water parable. If you have boiling water on a stove and you put a frog in that boiling water, it would immediately jump out. But if you put a frog in the water and slowly turn the heat up, the water will slowly boil the frog to death. In January 2002, the federal government signed into law The No Child Left Behind Act. This legislation was enacted so as to improve overall student performance and close the achievement gap between rich and poor students. However, this act is not designed to assess the technology skill obtainment students need to succeed today. This act does not teach a student to use the technology effectively. This act simply encourages school accountability, higher standards for students and educational measurements for achievement.

There needs to be a participative partnering between business, government, and education. There is agreed recognition that a problem exists. What our society requires is the creation of Technological-Immersion Centers. In the 2003 International Labour Conference Report, *Learning and training for work in the knowledge society*, it states that industrialized countries invest at least 30 times more per student in education and training than the least developed countries[54]. This conference concluded that many countries are taking steps to bridge the digital chasm, recognizing the "digital divide both between and within countries risks growing even wider unless serious efforts are undertaken nationally and internationally to reverse the trend." This report shared many examples of worldwide efforts in lifelong learning. At the European level, they identified the need of *all* citizens to develop a knowledge base that will help them find their way in the information society. It warned against the danger of social exclusion among some groups in society based on lack of knowledge. There was a call for Europe's education and training systems to adapt both to the demands of the knowledge society and to the need for an improved level and quality of employment. These entities were challenged to offer educational opportunities for differing knowledge levels and individuals at varying stages of their lives. For example, young people, unemployed adults and workers who are at risk of seeing their skills overtaken by rapid change. This new approach will include three main components: *the development of learning centers,* the promotion of new basic skills, in particular, information technologies; and the increased transparency of qualifications. Another example can be found in the Philippines where they have developed "Technical Education and Skills Development Authority (TESDA)" centers to develop world-class, technically skilled and educated workers with positive work values. The report clearly stated why these types of learning centers are so important:

> "The wealth of nations is increasingly based on the skills and knowledge of
> their workforces. A three-pronged strategy of education and training can be
> envisaged to meet the challenges of globalization and improved competitiveness,
> while reversing growing inequalities in labour market outcomes. The first prong
> should address the challenge of developing the knowledge and skills necessary
> for competition in tighter international markets. Access of all to lifelong-

learning is becoming a prerequisite in the developed countries as they endeavor to make their emerging knowledge and information society inclusive. In the developing countries, one of the most pressing needs is to build the basic "digital literacy" skills and ICT-related education and training that will allow these countries to access, harness, and ultimately innovate in new technologies for production and development. Widespread digital literacy must be based on a system of quality basic education. Wage and income inequalities increasingly reflect people's different endowments of education and skills. Therefore, equity-based policies that gives broad sections of the population access to education and training are also, in the long run, to contribute to reduced income inequalities within and between countries."

The development of Technology-Immersion Centers should be funded through partnerships in business, education, and government. These Centers would offer basic functional skills in technology such as how to use the Internet, how to communicate and navigate with e-mail correspondence, how to pay a bill on-line, how to e-commerce, and many other basic skills. The centers would need to offer one-on-one instruction. The fear of feeling "stupid" is real to the digital illiterate. Whether a youth or elderly person, the Technoism bug silences those who have a fear of the unknown or a fear of admitting to being a "techno-twit." As noted earlier in this book, there needs to be an acknowledgement of varying levels of technological achievement. The Technology-Immersion Centers would offer differing levels of technological training.

Our society, unless we take active steps towards technological literacy for all socio-economic levels, will suffer the consequences of an inadequate, market-driven, life-long learning initiative.

Organizational Assessment

Business and Industry

It is a common and often heard complaint in organizations today. Organizations purchase the latest and greatest technology and the investment ends up in storage or slowing down production for lack of knowledge on effective use of such technology. As an instructor, I have heard many adult students share stories of technological nightmares in workplaces today. Some complain of companies purchasing equipment with insistence that employees use the equipment even if the employees see it as a hindrance to their jobs. Others shake their heads as they share stories of company's purchasing the "latest" and "greatest" only to find the employees can't run the equipment or the equipment doesn't fit into the existing system while the equipment sits idle. Arnold Brown in the September-October, 2001 *Futurist*, observed:

> "In our organizations, we should resist the temptation to leap hastily and
> unthinkingly on the new technology bandwagon. In order to do that, there
> has to be a formal process for examining, analyzing and even anticipating
> relevant technologies and the impacts they could have. Large companies
> spend hundreds of millions of dollars on information technology systems
> and mere pennies on assessing the impacts on their people, their customers,
> and their organizations. The installation of any large-scale technology should
> not take place without such an assessment."

These sentiments are echoed in most classrooms that have adult students with full-time jobs in industry. Most individuals in business are well aware of the latest and newest management trends. Total Quality Management, Employee empowerment, Self-managed teams, and Systems thinking are just a few of business fads one has and does find in organizations today. One might assert that organizational technology investment without thorough assessment is another fad or trend of business today, a gift from the Trickster. As suggested for our society at large, organizations, too, need their own system of assessment and analysis. Technology should be viewed as one of many managerial tools and should be assessed to determine whether new technology actually contributes to the bottom-line. As we invest in training and education for employees today so they will become better problem-solvers and decision-makers, the newly-obtained skills of decision-making and critical thinking should be applied to technological purchases and advancement as well. Will there be a return-on-investment (ROI)?

It is suggested the following questions be asked in organizations before investing in technology:

1. Have we assessed the systemic impacts of the technology? The technology purchase should complement and transition into the system. Organizations are systems of interrelated components and it would be a grave mistake to purchase said equipment without thoroughly analyzing the system impact.

2.   Are we purchasing the equipment as a means to an end or because we are enthralled with the means or the finesse of the technological tool? Analyze the requirements of the organization that would make the technology a worthwhile investment. How do we envision the technology benefiting organizational goals? What problems will the technology help us solve? Have we conducted a cost-benefit analysis to determine if the technology meets our requirements? What decision criteria can we identify?

3.   Include employees in decision-making process. Employees know the system best and many will offer advice that could be more beneficial than any other form of analysis. Employee input must not be confused with employee resistance. Peter de Jager called this Rational or Irrational Resistance[26]. According to de Jager, rational resistance includes resisting because of lack of information or lack of training. Irrational Resistance describes those employees who refuse change and will never be convinced to do so. Employees need to be fully involved to see the big picture and offer constructive participation. Employees will resist change they don't understand and will fear the unknown. However, with training, education and employee involvement, organizational systems will benefit overall.

4.   What are the alternatives to investing in this equipment at this time? After we have determined the organizational objectives, we must determine the

alternative expenditures or changes that could meet our objectives. It may be wise to explore other organizations that have invested in such equipment. Spend as much time as needed to gather as much information as possible and research and assess the investment.

5. Weigh the risks, certainties, and uncertainties. For example, will the employees be able to function with the new equipment? Is that an uncertainty that must be addressed? An organization must estimate the likelihood of certain outcomes and uncertain outcomes. Does the purchase provide certain answers to certain problems? Are we confident the problem is not a symptom of a bigger problem? What if we take a risk with the equipment and find it is slowing down productivity or doesn't fit into our system? Will we feel a need to escalate commitment; maximizing our poor decision?

6. What are the costs of disruption of systems that will be attributed to the transition? Any major technological change will include a transitional period. Can these costs be justified? When looking at the big picture or system, ask if there is a pay-off for such investment even with potentially costly disruptions.

Technology is completely transforming how organizations function and interact with their environments. Employees have resisted technology for as long as there has been manual labor. Lord Byron, in 1812, sought to explain the Luddite rebellion to the House of Lords:

"My Lords, During the short time I recently passed in Nottinghamshire not twelve hours elapsed without some fresh act of violence;....I was informed that forty Frames had been broken the preceding evening. These machines....superseded the necessity of employing a number of workmen, who were left in consequence to starve. By the adoption of one species of Frame in particular, one man performed the work of many, and the superfluous labourers were thrown out of employment...The rejected workmen in the blindness of their ignorance, instead of rejoicing at these improvements in art so beneficial to mankind, conceived themselves to be sacrificed to improvements in mechanism" (as quoted by Leontief, 1991, p. 361).

Lord Byron's assertion is employees should rejoice at change that, in the long run, will benefit mankind. Technological paradox; it can destroy us without assessment but benefits mankind in the long run. The organization that assesses, analyzes, and considers the impact of technological investment will benefit as a whole and benefit all organizational members.

Educational Institutions

The consumer has spoken. Distance education is redefining the classroom we have known. The following recommendations offer guidance to new faculty for the appropriate utilization of distance learning as a learning tool:

1. Don't sacrifice substance for style. Although designing on-line courses may keep
   you in the technological loop and may demonstrate your graphics skills, substance
   can be lost when designing canned courses. It is possible to design courses on-line
   as long as the designer does not lose focus of course objectives, which should take
   precedence over style. Studies have shown that at university level, students feel
   the use of modern technology only provides an attractive presentation format but
   does little to enhance the learning.

2. There is something isolating with the communicative limitations of electronic
   interactions. A good rule of thumb when offering an on-line course is to insist on
   face-to-face meetings periodically during the semester. If distance makes this
   impossible, allow for video-conferencing or some type of "real-time"
   communication or direct contact with faculty.

3. Don't sacrifice your teaching philosophy because of Technoism. If you must
   participate in distance education, evaluate your teaching philosophy and
   determine how you will meet your personal teaching objectives if you teach
   courses on-line. Evaluate, question, share conflicted feelings with other faculty,
   and make an educated choice to remain true to your teaching philosophy.

4. Lastly, do not use technology for the sake of technology without evaluating the
   educational usefulness of such said technology. Will the technology enhance the
   learning experience? Will it facilitate learning of course objectives? Will it

provide reasonable return on investment; meaning will the investment prepare students adequately for the future? Does it meet faculty members' standards of quality? As we observed through the K-12 example, many administrators only evaluated the efficiency and effectiveness of classroom technology after purchase. At all educational levels, we are shifting from process to outcomes-based learning. If we rely on technology for this challenge, we must evaluate first before investing rather than allowing the Technoism choice, which is to invest first and evaluate later.

Individual Assessment

This book raises many red flags, alerting individuals in our technological world. Consumers need to be aware of the Trickster and Technoism at work in their lives.

➢ Purchases should be made carefully and the consumer should begin demanding more for their money. When something is outdated as soon as it leaves the store, it is not worth the investment. Question your purchases: Do I really need a cell phone with Internet capabilities, a two-way pager with e-mail access, and a personal digital assistant for when I am away from home or the office? Do I need a personal computer, scanner, digital camera, laptop, regular printer, a photograph printer, and a fax machine at home? Some individuals may indeed require these technological gadgets, but Technoism, or the pressure to be in the technological "in-group," must not influence the decision. Consumers need to make educated decisions and may consider learning from previous generations on the relationship between purchase, quality and service.

➢ Consumers must vocalize privacy concerns to their governmental elected officials. Citizens must speak out and demand more legislative protection from technological surveillance.

➤ Individuals also need to question the legitimacy of information found on the web and check it for historical accuracy. Many questionable web sites exist and the information is not based on fact but opinion.

➤ We also need to slow down and evaluate the impact technology has in our lives. Technology that is meant to un-stress our lives many times only makes our lives more chaotic. We must use sense in deciding how often we wish to be attainable and reachable by technology.

➤ Avoid isolating yourself from family, friends, and co-workers. The increasingly digitally-divided world we live in today isolates us from human interaction and face-to-face contact and increases stress levels of individuals. Once a day, when tempted to e-mail a friend, phone this person instead and set up a date for lunch.

➤ When using the Internet and e-mail, a user needs to exercise caution when downloading anything from the Internet and should never open suspicious e-mail attachments. The key is to be continually aware that one mistake can cause considerable, if not permanent, damage to your equipment.

➤ In the workplace, avoid visiting the Internet if possible and eliminate all jokes and suspect e-mail communications. The legal decisions continue to favor employers in these situations so therefore one must protect himself/herself from any misunderstandings.

A Final Word...............

John F. Kennedy once said that technology has no conscience of its own. What a visionary he was, because at no other time in our history has this been truer. Technology must be analyzed, assessed, and utilized so the impact on our lives is a positive one. By eliminating Technoism in our lives, we will be free to question the technological revolution and hold marketers and technology producers and merchants accountable. The Trickster loses power when exposed through marketing accountability. And his friend, Technoism ceases to exist when we assess the impact of technology. Assessment and analysis of the technology revolution allows for intelligent discussion on the potential unintentional consequences of technology development and utilization.

Technology has no conscience of its own, therefore we must fully assess the societal, organizational and institutional, and the individual impact of technology on our lives. We are at the crossroads of society and technology. We can choose which direction to go, the pace at which we wish to travel, and the quality of the journey.

Bibliography

1.   Amato, L. (June 25, 2001). X-ray vision. *Time*, v.157, No. 25, pp. 57-58.

2.   *American demographics.* v. 24, no. 3. "Can you set your VCR?" In R. Gardyn (ed).

3.   Baig, E.C., Stepanek, M., & Gross, N. (2000-2001). Privacy. *Business Ethics: Annual Editions.* Ed. Richardson, J.E., pp. 31-35.

4.   Bertman, S. (2000). *Cultural Amnesia.* Westport: Praeger.

5.   Blanchard, K. & Johnson, S. (1982). *The One-Minute Manager.* Berkley Books, NY

6.   Brown, A. (September-October, 2001). Sometimes the Luddites are right. *Futurist*, v.35, No. 5, pp. 38-41.

7.   *Business Week* (December 3, 2001). Giving it the old online try. pp. 76-80.

8.   *Business Week* (April 8, 1972). The debate over assessing technology: Congress wants to set up an office to evaluate the impact of new development. (1972). Available: www..wws.Princeton.edu/~ota/ns20/ota72_n.html Retrieved November 15, 2001.

9.   Bruzzese, A. (April 16, 2000). Companies sometimes monitor employees. *Journal and Courier*, p. E8. Lafayette, IN.

10.   Carr, S. (July 7, 2000). Many professors are optimistic on distance learning, survey finds. *The Chronicle of Higher Education, v. XLVI, No. 44*, p. 35.

11.   Challenger, J.A. (September-October, 2000). "24 trends reshaping the workplace." *Futurist*, v.34, No. 5.

12.   Coates, V. (September-October, 2001). The need for technology assessment. *Futurist*, V. 35, No. 5, pp. 42-43.

13.   Coates, V. (Fall, 1999). Technology forecasting and assessment in the United States: Statistics and prospects. *Futures Research Quarterly*, vv. 15, No. 3, pp. 5-25.

14.   Cohen, A. (July 2, 2001). Internet insecurity. *Time*, v. 157, no.26, pp. 44-51.

15.   Cohen, A. (February 26, 2001). In search of the Napster. *Time.* pp. 50-51.

16. Conklin, W. (Winter, 2001). The illusion of diversity: When ethics, technology and diversity clash. *The Diversity Factor,* v.9, no. 2, pp. 5-10.

17. Cornish, E., Wagner, C.G., Johnson, D., & Minerd, J. (January-February, 2000). "The opportunity century: 50 paths to success in the 21st century." *Futurist,* (v. 34, #1).

18. Crossman, W. (December, 1999). The coming age of talking computers. *The Futurist,* V. 33, No. 10, pp. 42-48.

19. Crutsinger, M. (September 17, 2000). "Computers now in over half of American homes." *South Bend Tribune,* (128th year, #223), p. B7. South Bend, IN.

20. Dannhauser, C.A.L. (December/January, 1999). "How'm I Doing?" *Working Woman.* p. 38.

21. Davis, B. (October, 2002). The technological divide: The power of language barriers. *Emerging Issues in Business and Technology Conference:* Myrtle Beach, SC.

22. Davis, B.(July, 2003). Distance learning: Educated choices or educational technoism? *The Association of Leadership Educators Conference:* Anchorage, AL.

23. Davis, B. & Crispo, A. (Spring, 2002) Technology in the classroom: bells and whistles of technoism or technoligcal tools to facilitate learning? ISETA Newsletter.

24. Davis, B.* & Crispo, A. (2001). Technoism: Suppressed skepticism and the echnology revolution. *2001 Proceedings of the Emerging Issues in Business and Technology Conference*: Myrtle Beach, SC. pp. 97-104.

25. Davis, C.K. (Winter, 2001). Planning for the unthinkable: IT Contingencies. National Forum, v.81, no. 1, pp.4-5.

26. De Jager, P. (May-June, 2001). Resistance to change: A new view of an old problem. *Futurist,* v. 35, no. 3, pp. 24-27.

27. DeTienne, K.B. (1996). Big brother or friendly coach? *Exploring your future: Living, learning and working in the information age.* Ed. E. Cornish. Pp. 62-66.

28. Dickson, P. (1998). *Slang. (*Simon & Schuster: New York).

29. Dunham, K.J. (January 17, 2001). Seeking the new, slimmed-down workday: 9-5. *Wall Street Journal, p. B1.*

30.   Enriquez, J. (2001). *As the future catches you.* (Crown Business Publishers: NewYork).

31.   Fahmy, S. (May 14, 2002). Hooked on E-mail, not grammar. *Journal and Courier.* Lafayette, IN.

32.   *Fast Company* (March, 2000). Technology insertion, pp. 212-219.

33.   Federal Trade Commission Privacy Report (June, 1998). *Privacy online: A report to congress,* http://www.ftc.gov/reports/privacy3/priv-23a.pdf

34.   Fishman, C. (April, 2001). But wait, you promised and believed us: Welcome to the real world. *Fast Company,* pp. 110-128.

35.   Fordahl, M. (April 28, 2002). High-tech support lacking. *South Bend Tribune,* p. B7. *Fortune: Technology guide.* (Summer, 2000). ISSN 0015-8259.

36.   *Fortune: Technology guide.* (Summer, 2000). ISSN 0015-8259

37.   Fosmoe, M. (May 30, 2002). Placing history in database debated. *South Bend Tribune, South Bend, IN.*

38.   Fussel, P. (1983). *Class: A guide through the American status system.* Touchstone: New York).

39.   *Futurist Update* (April, 2000). The internet vs. life. Retrieved: Futurist-update@wfs.org.

40.   Gidley, J. (2000). Unveiling the human face of university futures. In *The university in transformation: Global perspectives on the futures of the university.* Ed. Inayatullah, S. & Gidley, J. Westport, CT: Bergin & Garvey. pp. 235-245.

41.   Godin, S. (October, 2001). In my humble opinion…). *Fast Company,* pp. 86-89.

42.   Goodman, E. (May 22, 2002). Lack of trust can be by-product of new technology. *South Bend Tribune, South Bend, IN.*

43.   Goodman, E. (May 15, 2002). One more war: Defend simplicity. *South Bend Tribune, South Bend, IN* Boston, MA

44.   Gowen, S.G. (1992). *The politics of workplace literacy: A case study.* TeachersCollege Press: New York).

45.   Greenfield, K.T. (October 2, 2000). Meet the Napster. *Time.* Pp. 61-71.

46. Greengard, S. (1997-1998). Privacy: Entitlement or illusion? *Business Ethics: Annual Editions.* Ed. Richardson, J.E. pp. 42-49.

47. Hawkins, D. (November 10, 1997). Dangerous legacies. *Time.* pp. 99-101.

48. Henricks, M. (September 1, 2000). "High Speed Managers." *American Way.* pp. 128-131.

49. Herdman, R.C. (1993). "Adult literacy and new technologies: Tools for a lifetime." *U.S. Congress: Office of Technology Assessment.*

50. Higgins, L. (October 18, 2001). Use of technology in classrooms questioned. In *South Bend Tribune, South Bend, IN.* Knight Ridder Newspapers.

51. Hilsenrath, J. E. & Flint, J. (August 20, 2001). Consumers find fault with products of new economy. *Wall Street Journal,* p. A2.

52. Holmes, N. (2000). "Understanding Government Statistics." In R.S.Wurman (ed). *Understanding.* (R.R. Donnelly & Sons: New York).

53. Hymowitz, C. & Silverman, R. E. (January 16, 2001). Can workplace stress get any worse? *The Wall Street Journal.* pp. B1-B4.

54. International labour Conference (91st Session, 2003). *Learning and training for work in the knowledge society.* Report IV (1), International Labour Office, Geneva.

55. Jesdanun, A. (August 5, 2002). Spam fighters battling to a stalemate. *South Bend Tribune,* South Bend, IN.

56. Kadaba, L.S. (October 11, 2002). RU der? GR8 :). Wisconsin State Journal, p. D1.

57. Kessler, M. (May 7, 2002). Dude! Service slips at no. 1 pc maker Dell. *USA Today.*

58. Kirn, W. (March 5, 2001). Recession for dummies. *Time,* p. 57.

59. Kirsch, I. (1989). *Adult literacy: Helping Americans with midlevel skills prepare for the high level demands of tomorrow.* Educational Testing Service Development. (ERIC Document Reproduction Service No. ED308 473).

60. Kornblum, J. (April 17, 2001). Privacy tops Americans' list of tech concerns. *USA Today,* Lafayette, IN Journal and Courier, E1.

61. Leontief, W.W. (1991). The distribution of work and income. *Crisis in American*

Institutions. Ed.: Skolnick, J. H. & Currie, E. pp. 361-369.

62.   Louderback, J. (March, 2001). "America the wireless." *USA Weekend,* pp. 4-5.

63.   Manicas, P. (2000). Higher education at the brink. In *The university in transformation: Global perspectives on the futures of the university.* Ed. Inayatullah, S. & Gidley, J. Westport, CT: Bergin & Garvey. Pp. 31-40.

64.   Mazarr, M.J. (1999). *Global trends 2005.* (Palgrave Publishers: New York).

65.   McCall, A. (October 23, 2002). Report: Workers need more skills. *South Bend Tribune.* South Bend, IN. p. B1.

66.   McCarthy, M. J. (April 25, 2000). Your manager's policy on employee e-mail may have a weak spot. *Wall Street Journal.* P. A1.

67.   Meredith, G.E. (October, 1999). The demise of writing. *Futurist,* V. 33, No. 8, pp. 27-29.

68.   Morgan, M.G. (August 2, 1995). Death by congressional ignorance: How the Congressional office of technology assessment-small and excellent-was killed in the Frenzy of government downsizing. *Pittsburgh Post Gazette,* http://www.princeton,edu/~ota/ns20/ota95_n.html.

69.   Mossberg, W. (October, 25, 2001). "Technology grows up." *The Wall Street Journal,* pp. B1-B3, Wall Street Journal Marketplace.

70.   Nartker, D. (November 3, 2001). Sun-Times: Inside Comment.

71.   Neubauer, D. (2000). Will the future include us? Reflections of a practitioner of higher education. In *The university in transformation: Global perspectives on the futures of the university.* Ed. Inayatullah, S. & Gidley, J. Westport, CT: Bergin & Garvey. Pp. 41-54.

72.   Nicholas, P. (April 8, 2001). Congressional staffs struggle with flood of e-mails. *South Bend Tribune,* 12th year, No. 31, p. A5.

73.   Planet Papers (2001). *McCarthyism and its effects on America.* Retrieved 4/7/01: http://www.planetpapers.com/Assets/659.html.

74.   *Psychology Today, V. 35, No.4.* (August, 2002). Learn.com. p. 56.

75.   Putnam, R. D. (2000). *Bowling alone.* New York: Touchstone.

76.   Ramirez, C.E. (May 15, 2001). Soon, you'll be wearing a computer, too. *The Detroit News.* Lafayette Journal and Courier, Lafayette, IN. p. E1.

77. Recer, P. (March 28, 2001). "Americans Are Sleep-deprived, Drowsy: Survey." *South Bend Tribune*. p. A3. South Bend, IN.

78. Renn, O. (Fall, 1999). Participative technology assessment: Meeting the challenges of uncertainty and ambivalence. *Futures Research Quarterly*, V. 15, No.3, pp. 81-97.

79. Reuters (October 12, 2000). Internet gap to continue, study finds. *Los Angeles Times*. p. C8. Los Angeles, CA.

80. Robinson, E. T. (November, 2000). The human component. *Syllabus*, pp. 54-65.

81. Rosen, R. (2000). *Global literacies*. (Simon & Schuster: New York).

82. Schulman, M. (1996-2000). Little brother is watching you. *Business Ethics: Annual Editions*. Ed. Richardson, J.E. pp. 35-39,

83. *Science and Technology Advice to the U.S. Congress:* Briefing Notes on a workshop, Washington, D.C., June 14, 2001.

84. Simpkins, S. (2001). A story fram'd in sport: Narrative tricks and wordsworth's ruined cottage complex. In *Trickster: Dance of differentiation and ambivalence*, pp. 79-96. Ed. Spinks, C. W, Atwood Publishing: Madison, WI.

85. Skolnik, M. (2000). The virtual university and the professoriate. In *The university in transformation: Global perspectives on the futures of the university*. Ed. Inayatullah, S. & Gidley, J. Westport, CT: Bergin & Garvey. Pp. 55-67.

86. Solomon, J. (1988). *The signs of our time.* (St. Martin's Press: Los Angeles).

87. *South Bend Tribune* (September 11, 2002). Letter from long ago, p. A6.

88. *South Bend Tribune* (February 12, 2001). Gene map raises fear of discrimination, p. A3.

89. Stewart, M.E. (March, 2001). Distance learning: Tradeoffs and ambivalence. *Teaching Professor, V. 15, No. 3*, pp. 1-3.

90. Stockall, N. (2001). The expert pilot: Trickster extraordinaire. In *Trickster: Dance of differentiation and ambivalence*, pp. 119-125. Ed. Spinks, C. W, Atwood Publishing: Madison, WI.

91. Taylor, C. (December 4, 2000). "Digital divide: So close and yet so far." *Time*, pp. 121-125.

92. Thurow, L. (1998). "Changing the name of capitalism." In R. Gibson (Ed). *Rethinking the future*, pp. ix. (Nicholas Brealey Publshing: London).

93. Veverka, A. (October 27, 2002). Victims of a mill death. *The Charlotte Observer,* v. 132, no. 300. pp. 1-11.

94. Von Holzen, R. (November, 2000). A look at the future of higher education. *Syllabus.* Pp. 56-65.

95. Wright, G. (December 25, 2001). Caught in the net. *Journal and Courier.* Lafayette, IN.

96. Yaukey, J. (October 16, 2001). Hacker havoc. *Lafayette Journal and Courier.* Lafayette, IN. p. E1.

Note: Some portions of this book have previously been printed for conference presentations. Every attempt has been made to give full credit to all references.

About the Author

Beverly Davis is an Associate Professor of Organizational Leadership in the School of

Technology at Purdue University at a statewide technology location in South Bend, IN.

She is available for speaking engagements.

bjdavis@pusb.iusb.edu

574-237-6581

www.southbend.tech.purdue.edu/bevbio.htm

Printed in the United States
16149LVS00003B/139-168